AF559833

Farm Crisis

The Way Out

The Author

Dr. Parveen Kumar completed his Doctoral degree in Agricultural Extension Education from Sher-e-Kashmir University of Agricultural Sciences and Technology of Jammu. He also has a Post Graduate Diploma in Rural Development from Indira Gandhi National Open University. This is his second book, the first one being **Agricultural Extension: The Changing Structure.** He has published various research papers besides having many review papers on social aspects too; and is presently engaged as a Senior Research Fellow in a National Initiative on Climate Resilient Agriculture.

Farm Crisis

The Way Out

— *Author* —
Dr. Parveen Kumar

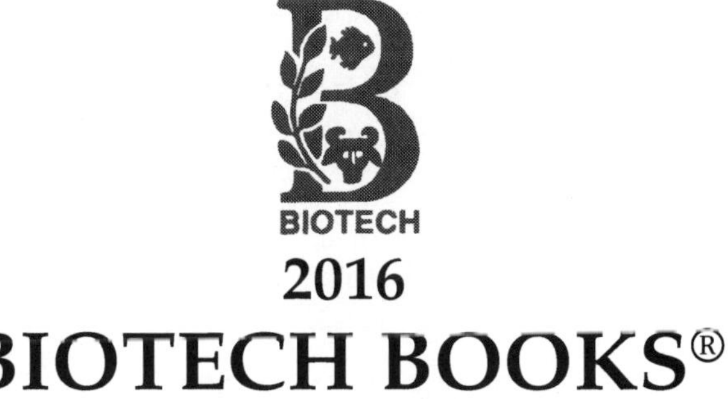

2016
BIOTECH BOOKS®

ISBN 978-81-7622-340-9

Published by: **BIOTECH BOOKS®**
4762-63/23, Ansari Road, Darya Ganj,
New Delhi - 110 002
Phone: +91-011-23262132
E-mail: biotechbooks@yahoo.co.in

Typeset at:**Classic Computer Services**
Delhi - 110 035

Digitally Printed at : **Replika Press Pvt. Ltd**

PRINTED IN INDIA

Dedicated to the farming community that feeds the nation

'Our salvation can only come through the farmer.
Neither the lawyers, nor the doctors
nor the rich landlords are going to secure it'

— Mahatma Gandhi

ACKNOWLEDGEMENT

I place on record my deep sense of gratitude to my esteemed teachers Dr G. R. Bhagat, Dr. Rakesh Nanda, Dr. S. K. Kher, Dr. Rajinder Peshin Dr. P. S. Slathia, Dr Nafees Ahmed and Dr. Poonam Parihar for their blessings and inspiration. I also take this opportunity to extend my gratitude to Dr. M. S. Nain Sr. Scientist, Indian Agriculture Research Institute, New Delhi. I extend my thanks to my colleagues Dr. Liaqat Ali, Dr. Vijay Kumar, Dr. Yogesh Kumar, Mr. Rakesh Bhagat and Mr. Manzar Masood for their support and encouragement while writing this book.

My better half; my wife Rita, her support all through the years, I have been with her has been utmost. She also deserves appreciation. Duty bound, I also acknowledge the contribution of my father Sh. Doulat Ram and with great regards, I pay homage to my mother Late Smt. Pushpa Devi.

I do not claim that the contents of the book are exclusive of me; but the information contained in the book has been gathered from different sources. I do here sincerely thank all those researchers, academicians and the different agencies whose work I have quoted here and also to those whom I could not. All this was done to bring out a comprehensive picture of the various challenges confronting the agricultural sector that have taken a crisis like situation. I also hope that through this book, the issues would receive greater attention from the concerned stakeholders.

Last but in no way the least, I also appreciate the efforts of Mr. Sunil Mittal of M/S Biotech Publishers, Daryaganj, New Delhi in bringing out this book.

Dr. Parveen Kumar

PREFACE

Agriculture sector is passing through tough times. No longer is it considered as a noble profession. While production has increased, the farms have become inefficient. The farm sector depicts a grim scenario. The soils have degraded, mechanization has been confined only to tractorization, water availability is on the decrease, food grains are being wasted, the climate change is threatening it and the never ending fragmentation of land has lead to a crisis like situation in this sector.

The book is an attempt to present in detail the various challenges that the agriculture sector is exposed to. The first chapter of the book elaborates on how agriculture till date has largely been a culture misunderstood. It dwells at length the fate of the farmer over the years, the still to be achieved agricultural growth rate, the story of grain drain, the minimum support prices and the agriculture subsidies. The second chapter of the book discusses in detail the various issues facing the agriculture sector. It focuses on important aspects of agriculture more specific to India such as declining share of investment in agriculture, the land use dynamics, declining size of operational holdings, low level of farm mechanization and food processing. The third chapter of the book is devoted to rainfed agriculture. The chapter discusses at length the importance of the rainfed agriculture in the global as well as national economy, the constraints of agricultural production in this handicapped zone and the strategies for overcoming various constraints. A report of the Institute of Applied Manpower Research (IAMR), a part of the planning commission said that on an average more than 2000 farmers are losing main cultivator status every single day for the last 20 years. The fourth chapter is dedicated to the cause of these helpless farmers. Public Distribution system in India has become a Public Diversion System. A series of reports have revealed sorry state of affairs and the mess prevailing in the system. The fifth chapter of the book explores some global findings about this system and the various alternatives to this highly corrupted distribution system. A strong extension system and a dedicated pool of extension professional are the back bone of any agricultural development programme. The public extension system in the recent times has come under serious attack due to its inability to provide relevant and timely information to the farming community. Chapter six of the book has been kept exclusively for how to revitalize the extension services, how the weaknesses can be removed and how the paradigm changed to rope in the private players and building partnerships to provide the extension services to the farmers. Poverty all over the globe has become a shame and our country is no exception. We make tall claims of being one of the largest economies but unfortunately after more than sixty years of attaining independence, we still suffer from hunger and poverty. Although poverty has declined over the years but still a lot needs to be done. The seventh chapter of the book carries the debate on agriculture and poverty It describes the need to ensure farmer security first and then to talk of food security. At present, throughout the world there exists a great concern about the effect of climate change as climate is one of the main determinants of agricultural production. It has caused variability in yield of crops and has a profound effect on livestock, forestry, fisheries and water resources. Chapter eighth of the book is an appraisal of how agriculture affects climate and in turn is itself affected by it. It describes how the agriculture, livestock, the water bodies and the aquatic ecosystem is being affected and the measures to lessen the effects of the global climate change. Over the years various agricultural practices have lead to a crisis like situation in agriculture sector. Chapter nine of the book summarizes how agriculture crisis can be overcome by different approaches like the farming system approach, farm mechanization, cooperative farming and farmer's mobilization. Sustainability today is the need and cry of the hour.

Chapter ten of the book is exclusively on sustainable agriculture. It describes how the chemical intensive cultivation has made this sector sustainable and how the sustainability can be achieved by following the integrated techniques like IPM, IWM, INM, organic farming, Indigenous technical knowledge. No single solution to achieve food security for all will suffice. Many significant changes are required. Agriculture needs some out of box solutions. Chapter eleven of the book mentions some out of box solutions like interlinking of rivers, using non conventional sources like the solar power, the wind power in the agriculture sector and the use of nano technology in agriculture.

An earnest effort has been made through this book to present a holistic picture of the challenges that ail agriculture in general and to India in particular and the ways the things can be set right. Acknowledgement is on the records for all those learned personalities who have been quoted in this book, and also to those who could not be, for it was their intellect which facilitated me in writing this book.

With the hope that the book will become a valuable source of information for the policy makers, the planners, the research scientists and the scholars to reorient their efforts in making agriculture environmentally sustainable and economically more remunerative.

Dr. Parveen Kumar

CONTENTS

Acknowledgement *vii*

Preface *ix*

Abbreviations *xvii*

List of Tables *xix*

1. Agriculture: The Culture Misunderstood **1**

1.1 The Fate of the Farmer 3
1.2 HUNGaMA 4
1.4 The Still Illusive Growth Rate 6
1.5 The Invisible Partners 9
1.6 The Problem of Grain Drain 10
1.7 Minimum Support Prices and the Farmer's Dilemma 12
1.8 Agriculture Credit 14
1.9 Agricultural Subsidies 16

2. Major Issues in Indian Agriculture **25**

2.1 Declining Share of Investment in Agriculture 26
2.2 Land Use Dynamics 27
2.3 Declining Size of Operational Holdings 28
2.4 The Low Yields 29

2.6 Rainfed Agriculture 29
2.7 Food Processing 29
2.8 Wastage in different Crops 32
2.9 Grain Drain 33

3. The Handicapped Zone: Rainfed Agriculture **34**
3.1 Resource Conservation Technologies 36
3.2 Diversification with High Value Crops 37
3.3 Modification of Agronomic Approaches 37
3.4 Suitable Varieties for Rainfed Areas 38

4. The Helpless 2000 Plus **41**
4.1 Attracting and Retaining Youth in Agriculture (ARYA) 43
4.2 Creating Agripreneurs 44

5. Public Distribution System: Causality of Mismanagement **48**
5.1 Different Alternatives to the PDS that can be Tried 50

6. Revitalizing Extension Services **56**
6.1 Conventional vs. Agriculture Innovation Systems Approach 58
6.2 Innovations in Agricultural Extension 59
6.3 Revitalizing Extension Services 66

7. Agriculture and Poverty Reduction **70**
7.1 Poverty Trend and Food Grain Availability 70
7.2 The Food Grain Scenario in India 72
7.3 Millennium Development Goals (MDGs) 72
7.4 Reducing Poverty via Agriculture 73
7.5 Right to Food and Food Security Act 75
7.6 Food Security Act: Some Concerns 75
7.7 Food Security and Population 76

8. Fighting Climate Change **78**
8.1 How Agriculture Contributes to Climate Change 80
8.2 Effect of Climate Change on Agriculture 81
8.3 Tackling Climate Change 84

9. Agriculture Crisis: The Way Out **89**
9.1 Diversification 89
9.2 Focusing Small farmers: 94

9.3 Doing away with Yield Gaps 97
9.4 Cropping Intensity 98
9.5 Use of Modern Inputs 98
9.6 Farm Mechanization 99
9.7 Augmenting Irrigation Capacity 101
9.8 Increasing Water Use Efficiency 101
9.9 Food Processing 102
9.10 Preventing Grain Drain 103
9.11 Utilizing Wasteland 103
9.12 Agriculture Infrastructure 104
9.13 Genetically Modified Crops 108
9.14 Crop Insurance 111
9.15 Promoting Agri-Tourism 115
9.16 Mobilizing Farmer Community 118
9.17 Cooperative Farming 120
9.18 The Orphan Crops 121
9.19 Agri-preneurship 123

10. Sustainable Agricultural Development **126**
10.1 The Need for Sustainability 126
10.2 Sustainable Development 128
10.3 Different Aspects of Sustainable Agriculture 130
10.4 Paid Ecological Services 134
10.5 Family Farms 136
10.6 Protecting Farmers' Rights: PPV and FRA 138
10.7 Futures Market 140

11. Out of Box Solutions **143**
11.1 Interlinking of Rivers 143
11.2 Nanotechnology 144
11.3 Using Renewable Energy Sources 148
11.4 Using Space for Agriculture 150
11.6 Urban Agriculture 152
11.7 Bottlenecks Analysis and Interventions in Agriculture 160

References **161**

Index **171**

ABBREVIATIONS

AIDIS: All India Debt and Investment Survey
BRICS: Brazil, Russia, India, China, South Africa
CACP: Commission on Agricultural Costs and Prices
CAMPA: Compensatory Afforestation Fund Management and Planning Authority
CAST: Council on Agriculture, Science and Technology
CCI: Confederation of Indian Industries
CGIAR: Consultative Group for International Agricultural Research
CIP: Central Issue Price
COAG: Council of Australian Governments
CSTEP: Center for study of Science Technology and Policy
DESA: Department of Economics and Social Affairs
FAO: Food and Agriculture Organization
FDI: Foreign Direct Investment
GCA: Gross Cultivated Area
GFU: Global Facilitation Unit
GDP: Gross Domestic Product
HUNGaMA: Hunger and Malnutrition

IFFCO: Indian Farmer Fertilizer Cooperation Ltd.
IFPRI: International Food Policy Research Institute
IKSL: IFFCO Kissan Sanchar Ltd.
INM: Integrated Nutrient Management
IPM: Integrated Pest Management
IWM: Integrated Weed Management
IWEA: Indian Wind Energy Association
KCC: Kissan Credit Cards
FAO: Food and Agricultural Organization
ICAR: Indian Council of Agricultural Research
ICESCR: International Covenant on Economic, Social and Cultural Rights
ICRISAT: International Center for Research in Semi Arid Tropics
IFAD: International Fund for Agricultural Development
IPCC: Intergovernmental Panel on Climate Change
IPGRI : International Plant Genetic Resource Institute
IPSARD: Institute of Policy and Strategy for Agricultural and Rural Development
IMAR: Institute of Men power and Applied Research
NARS: National Agricultural Research System
MGNREGA: Mahatma Gandhi National Rural Employment Guarantee Act
MSP: Minimum Support Prices
NABARD: National Bank for Agriculture and Rural Development
NCAER: National Council for Applied Economic Research
NSSO: National Sample Survey Organization
PEG: Private Entrepreneurs Guarantee
SAU: State Agricultural Universities
USAID: United States Agency for International Development
USDA: United States Department of Agriculture
WIC: Women, Infant and Children

LIST OF TABLES

Table 1: State-wise Number of Farmers' Suicides in India (1995-2010) 5
Table 2: Budget Outlay on Agriculture and Allied Activities (Rs crores) in Various Five Year Plans 8
Table 3: Relative Proportion of Borrowing from each Agency to Total Borrowings of Cultivators 15
Table 4: Vital Statistics about PACS 16
Table 5: Agriculture Subsidies (in US $) in Selected Countries (1999) 18
Table 6: Central Subsidy on all Fertilizers (in Rupees crore) 19
Table 7: Indian Population vs. Food Grains Production 26
Table 8: Land Use Dynamics in India in Million Hectares (m ha) 28
Table 9: Percentage of different Size of Holdings as per Agriculture Census 2005-06 28
Table 10: Area, Production and Yield of different Crops in India (2011-12) 30
Table 11: Level of Mechanization of different Farm Operations in Indian Agriculture 31

Table 12:	Level of Food Processing in India	31
Table 13:	Per cent Wastage in Various Crops	32
Table 14:	Important Characteristics of Predominantly Rainfed and Irrigated Areas	36
Table 15:	Number of Cultivators and Labourers	42
Table 16:	Agricultural Production and Workforce	42
Table 17:	Percentage of Farm Households Accessing Information on Modern Agricultural Technologies from different Sources	58
Table 18:	Various Public Private Partnerships (PPP)	61
Table 19:	Some ICT based initiatives in India	62
Table 20:	Various Expert Systems being put in use in Agriculture and related sectors	63
Table 21:	Poverty Trend in India from 1973-74 to 2004-05	71
Table 22:	Trend in per Person Net Cereal Availability (in gm)	71
Table 23:	Calories and Protein Intake of the Rural Poorest Thirty per cent Households	72
Table 24:	Incidence of Hunger and Poverty by Farm Size in Rural India	74
Table 25:	Expected Number of Undernourished Population (in millions) Incorporating the Effects of Climate	79
Table 26:	Major Green House Gases (GHG's) and their Principal Sources	80
Table 27:	Abundance and Lifetime of Greenhouse Gases in the Atmosphere	81
Table 28:	Effect of Mechanization on different Aspects of Crop Production	99
Table 29:	Status of Orphan Crops in India	123
Table 30:	Bottlenecks Analysis and Possible Interventions in Food Crops	157
Table 31:	Bottlenecks Analysis and Interventions in Livestock	158
Table 32:	Bottlenecks Analysis and Interventions in Horticulture	159
Table 33:	Bottlenecks Analysis and Interventions in Sericulture	160

Chapter 1

AGRICULTURE: THE CULTURE MISUNDERSTOOD

It has been rightly said, 'lands are those assets, not inherited by our ancestors, but borrowed from our children'. This is the basis on which Indian farmers serve as custodians to lands striving to nurture them to be handed over to their children's in good condition (Reddy Narayana, 2011). After our parents the most affectionate thing for anybody in our country particularly for farmers is the land. It is the land that produces food, holds rainwater underground, helps vegetation to grow and produce oxygen for the humanity to survive. Land is the pride possession of the farmer and for him it is his religion, asset and everything. Several ancient texts clearly show that the farmers were held in high esteem million years ago. In the Ramayna, Lord Rama had advised his younger brother Bharata, to ensure that all those engaged in agriculture and animal husbandry receive his special attention. The world attains happiness and prosperity only on the foundation of Varta. The varta includes crop, animal husbandry and trade.

Agriculture in India is more than just a field work. For majority of them it is a way of life. Most of human history, we have lived our daily lives in a close relationship with the land. Agriculture is such embedded in our culture that many festivals are associated with it and these festivals strengthen the bonds of love and brotherhood between different communities. While some festivals mark the beginning of the harvesting season some are a way of thanking the mother earth for obliging with its fertility and diversity. Such is the diversity that even tastes of water changes after every kilometer. Almost every region has its own festival that has a special significance for agriculture. The festival of 'Baisakhi' in the month of April and celebrated with fervor and gaiety in northern parts of India marks the harvest of Rabi crops. The 'Makar Sankranti' signifies the northward journey of the sun indicating the days getting longer and warmer. The festival of Pola in Maharashtra celebrated in the holy month of Shravan is the day when farmers worship their bulls thanking them for the hard work and efforts they put in the fields. The 'Onam' in Kerala is a festival of reaping the harvest. The festival longs ten days. Boat rowing crews and the beating of drums by the crews adds attraction to the festival. 'Letri' in the hilly areas of Jammu and Kashmir is also a harvest festival associated with the cutting of grass and storing it for fodder purpose to be used in the dry period/off season. There are so many other festivals like 'Matu Puja', in Chhattisgarh, 'Amongmong' in Nagaland and Bhadrapadaa Anbaji fair in Gujarat. All these are a reflection of the beliefs, values and traditions of the masses of India associated with agriculture

Agriculture envisages the expansion of a new form of food production and consumption founded on more ecological principles and in harmony with the cultures, knowledge and collective capacities of the producers themselves. Our modern lifestyles and economies would need six or eight earths if the entire world's population adopted our profligate ways. We are rendering our own world inhospitable and so risk losing what it means to be human: unless we make substantial changes. As against the three fold increase in population, we have achieved more than fourfold increase in production. Indian agriculture has the advantage of 52 per cent of cultivable land and a plethora of climatic conditions. India enjoys sunshine round the year and it is the world's best country to grow crops throughout the year. India has the second largest area under cultivation, Highest area under irrigation 55.8 million hectare (China has 54.5 million hectare under irrigation and United States has 22.4 million hectares under irrigation), third in food grains production, world's largest user of fertilizers (11 per cent of world's dosage), first in production of Pulses, second in production of cereals like Wheat and second in production of vegetables next only to China. This has been achieved through a favourable interplay of infrastructure, technology, extension, policy support backed by strong political will (Planning commission, 2008). Besides we are also first in livestock population, 18 per cent of world's cattle population with 13 per cent of world's total milk production is contributed by India.

The Indian Council of Agricultural Research has been leading from the front for agricultural development through research and technology generation and its transfer through various programmes that has enabled the country to increase the production of food grains by 4 times, horticultural crops by 6 times, fish by 9 times (marine 5 times and inland 17 times), milk 6 times and eggs 27 times since 1950-51, thus making a visible impact on the national food and nutritional security (Kokate and Srinath, 2012). But inspite of achieving all this, something appears going wrong with our agricultural production and food management systems. Despite great progress in increasing productivity in recent decades, hundreds of millions of people remain hungry and malnourished, and further millions suffer for eating too much food of the wrong sort. The condition of the farming community which forms the backbone of the economy is getting worsened day by day. Here a few facts are mentioned

1.1 The Fate of the Farmer

Farmers till the soil in the scorching heat to produce food for the millions of us. But farmers still are destitute in their own country. Agriculture once considered as a noble profession is now largely seen as a passage to poverty, indebtedness and suicides. The stark reality is that farmer only has to produce; he cannot seek what he wants. Others have the right to determine what is good for him. He buys inputs at the highest prices but often sells the output at the lowest price. Being a farmer today means only to serve others. The various policies of the government have led to the pauperization of peasantry. Government announces the Minimum Support Price which even does not covers the total cost of cultivation. Center for Sustainable Agriculture in Andhra Pradesh, a major rice growing state in the country calculated the cost of cultivation of Paddy in 2011-12. The cost of cultivation worked out to be 1800 per quintal whereas the MSP announced was only 1080. Such is the plight of the farmers that the Paddy growing farmers of Andhra Pradesh observed a crop holiday to protest the increase in input costs. The rising input costs have rendered the farming non viable. About three lakh acres of land were left fallow in four districts of Andhra Pradesh (Kang, B 2012). This has resulted in widening disparity between the rural and urban incomes. When it comes to marketing the condition is still the same as was quoted by W. H. Moreland in **'From Akbar to Aurangzeb'.** Commenting on the agrarian system of Mughal India he had said that Peasant is the last person to benefit from price rise while he is the first to suffer from price fall. Nothing remarkable has changed since the days of Moreland. A large number of middlemen and commission agents in the retail market work in tandem to make huge profits from the farmers produce. On the name of liberalization and economic reforms farmers are forced to sell their land for Special Economic Zones. Those who resist the move are forcefully evicted. The financial institutions are still reluctant to grant loans to them. Even the compulsory priority sector lending targets are not achieved by the Banks. The crop insurance front also presents a grim picture. Insurance is an uncommon practice with only 14 per cent of the large farmers, only 2 per cent of the sub marginal farmers and 5 per cent of the small farmers had crop insurance. The son of a farmer is not interested in carrying forward his traditional occupation. Research institutions are not delivering the results expected of them. Funding for publicly provided research and extension has not kept pace with the increasing need for such support.

1.2 HUNGaMA

Former Indian Prime Minister Late Shri Lal Bahadur Shastri had once said that all Indians should fast week once a week so that another might get a meal. That very spectre of food insecurity stills looms large over the Indian population. To what former Prime minister of India Dr. Manmohan Singh described as a national shame, the findings of HUNGaMA Survey Report 2011, which said that in 100 focus districts located in six states, 42 per cent of children under five are underweight and 59 per cent are stunted.The report of National Crime records bureau 2009 also came out with a shocking revelation. It put the number of suicides in the year 2009 at 17,368 (Kumar, N., 2011).

The report further said that the suicides are not region specific but are spread across India. 46 farmers commit suicide every day even as the

Table 1: State-wise Number of Farmers' Suicides in India (1995-2010)

State	*Male*	*Female*	*Total*
Andhra Pradesh	25,462	5,658	31,120
Arunachal Pradesh	158	30	188
Assam	3,302	264	3,566
Bihar	1,058	177	1,235
Chattisgarh	11,686	2,654	14,340
Goa	163	7	170
Gujarat	7,340	1,443	8,783
Haryana	2,639	181	2,820
Himachal Pradesh	560	71	631
Jammu and Kashmir	159	28	187
Jharkhand	791	47	838
Karnataka	28,739	6,314	35,053
Kerala	17,617	1,290	18,907
Madhya Pradesh	21,038	5,684	26,722
Maharashtra	44,837	5,644	50,481
Manipur	15	5	20
Meghalaya	115	19	134
Mizoram	52	5	57
Nagaland	20	3	23
Odisha	3,856	604	4,460
Punjab	1,248	15	1,263
Rajasthan	8,063	1,202	9,265
Sikkim	289	88	377
Tamil Nadu	11,252	2,623	13,875
Tripura	731	404	1,135
Uttar Pradesh	7,777	1,593	9,370
Uttrakhand	252	66	318
West Bengal	15,470	3,861	19,331
Total	**21,4689**	**39,980**	**25,4669**

Of the total 2,54,669 cases of farmers suicide 2,14,689 were male and 39,980 were females. Among the top five states, the state of Maharashtra was leading the table with 50,481 suicide cases followed by Karnataka having 35,053 suicides, Andhra Pradesh (31,120 cases), Madhya Pradesh (26,722 cases) and West Bengal having 19,331 cases during the reference years.

packages are rolled out in a bid to bail out the debt ridden community from the crisis. The Nutrition Barometer Launched by two NGO's 'World vision and Save the Children' that assess the government's political legal and financial commitments towards tackling the scourge in 36 countries which are home to 90 per cent of world's malnourished children says that in India every day 5000 children die largely due to causes that are preventable like malnutrition and lack of a proper diet. On the Nutrition Barometer the adjoining states like Pakistan, Nepal and Bangladesh have performed better then India. Indian performance is similar to Democratic republic of Kongo and Yemen which too are weak performers. According to a USAID document (1995), "Global agriculture currently produces ample calories and nutrients to provide all the world's population healthy and productive lives". The problem lies in the distribution also. Food is not distributed equally to regions, countries, households and individuals. Improved access to food through increased agricultural productivity and incomes is essential to meet the food needs of the world's growing population.

1.4 The Still Illusive Growth Rate

From food shortages and imports to self sufficiency and export, from subsistence farming to intensive and technology led cultivation, today India is the front ranking producer of many crops in the world ushered in through green, white, blue and yellow revolution. Agriculture contributes about 14.2 per cent of Gross Domestic Product (Anonymous, 2012). During eleventh five year plan, 4 per cent GDP growth rate was expected from agriculture which turned out to be 4.5 per cent (2007-08) to 5.4 per cent (2010-11) (Rao and Mishra, 2011). This should not come as a surprise, given the steady decline in the share of public investment in agriculture (from 20.5 per cent in 2004/05 to 17.6 per cent in 2008/09) and the low public investment in agricultural research and development *i.e.* 0.5 per cent of agricultural gross domestic product (GDP) as against the norm of 1 per cent recommended by the Indian Council of Agricultural Research affecting technological progress. That is one of the reasons why the Indian agriculture sector remains one of the least productive in the world (Binswanger-Mkhize and Parikh 2012).

Second is the decline of share of agricultural growth in country's GDP. Although a falling share of agriculture in GDP, from 28 per cent in 1996-

97 to 14.2 per cent in 2010-11 is indicative of structural transformation of the economy, the sector continues to be the predominant source of livelihood for more than half the nation's total labor force and more than two-thirds of the rural labor force (India, Ministry of Finance 2011). What is more disturbing is that we are going to achieve 4 per cent growth rate even when agriculture does not grows at the rate of 4 per cent. This means we would have growth but not inclusive growth because 52 per cent of peoples still depend on agriculture (Sharma, R. 2012). There also prevails a huge disparity in growth rates among different states of the country. While at the national level we are struggling to achieve 4 per cent growth rate, in state like Gujarat agriculture sector grew at a rate of 10.2 per cent between 2000-01 and 2008-09. In the same period the agricultural growth rate in Uttar Pradesh and West Bengal was 2.2 per cent and 2.4 per cent, respectively. What is needed today is enhancing of public investment in agriculture. Together with private investment, the overall capital formation in agriculture is now about 12 per cent of agriculture GDP which is the highest in the last 25 years (Planning Commission 2008). By the end of the Eleventh Plan, this is expected to go over 16 per cent- necessary for sustaining 4 per cent annual growth in agriculture GDP. The percentage of agriculture and allied activities investment to total plan outlay and actual plan expenditure has to show a increasing trend which at present is declining trend with some exceptions. It has shown lesser variation from first plan to eighth plan period. This is also necessary for improving agriculture infrastructure. More needs to be invested in agricultural research and development. It has enormous potential to provide solutions to the persisting problems. To meet the social goals and reaching the unreached, a strong public Research and Development system is needed.

More public investment is needed in the rainfed and backward areas. Many of the ills of the agriculture sector, namely, low productivity, low employment opportunities and inadequate infrastructure are attributed to inadequate and progressive decline in the public investment in agriculture. India has made rapid strides in food grain production as also in the production of fruits and vegetables. However, the lack of adequate post-harvest management and marketing facilities have resulted in glut in the market and consequent distress sales as also heavy post harvest losses to the tune of 25-30 per cent. Taking the cue from China, value addition to agricultural products should be taken on priority through establishing agro-processing units in rural areas especially for export oriented products as we are exporting less than 2 per cent of agricultural products as value added. Although we are second largest producer of fruits and vegetables, yet we are processing 2.2 per cent of their production against 65-70 per cent in developed nations and 23 per cent in China. The public investment intensity of Research and Extension is only 0.4 per cent as against 0.6 per cent in the developing countries and more than 1 per cent globally. ICAR-SAUs system has developed several improved region-specific technologies over the years and these have good potential to increase income and employment and make farming a profitable source of livelihood. There is a need of developing appropriate mechanism and providing support for their adoption.

Table 2: Budget Outlay on Agriculture and Allied Activities (Rs crores) in Various Five Year Plans

Plan	*Total Plan Outlay*	*Agriculture and Allied Activities*	*Percentage of Agriculture and Allied Activities to Total Plan Outlay*
Ist Plan	2378	354	14.9
2nd Plan	4500	510	11.3
3rd Plan	7500	1086	14.5
Annual Plan	6665	1037	15.6
IVth Plan	15902	2728	17.2
Vth Plan	39322	4766	12.1
Annual Plan	12601	1815	14.4
VIth Plan	97500	12539	12.9
VIIth Plan	180000	22233	12.4
Annual Plan	137034	19200	14.0
VIIIth Plan	434100	63642	14.7
IXth Plan	859200	42462	4.9
Xth Plan	1525639	58933	3.9
XIth Plan	3644718	136381	3.7

1.5 The Invisible Partners

The history of agriculture has clearly established the fact that settlement around major rivers (Yellow, Nile, Ganges etc.) of the world led to the beginning of raising crops and animals on the farm lands mainly due to insistence of women. But for their role, perhaps man would have still remained simply a gatherer or hunter (Paroda, 2012). As producers, workers and marketers, women are the bedrock of agriculture in the developing world. Their continued marginalization has inevitably contributed to slowing the World's progress in overcoming poverty and hunger. Agricultural growth remains seriously underexploited as a means to promote development even though it is known to reduce poverty by twice the rate of other non-agricultural sectors. Especially smallholder agriculture is underperforming because women, who represent as many as half the farmers in many poor countries, cannot access the technology and other inputs they need to be fully productive. They are involved in all aspects of agriculture, from crop selection to land preparation, to seed selection, planting, weeding, pest control, harvesting, crop storage, handling, marketing, and processing. Despite this much of the contribution of women in the food production system their role as food producers and providers is yet to be given effective recognition. Though women in India contribute most of the labour in agriculture, only a miniscule seven per cent have any legal control on agricultural land (Haque and Rake, 2012) Available figures show that only 5 per cent of extension services have been addressed to rural women, while no more than 15 per cent of the world's extension agents are women. In addition, most extension services are focused on cash crops rather than food and subsistence crops, which are the primary concern of women farmers and the key to food security. This is true for Indian agriculture also. High illiteracy rates and poor living conditions among rural women, lack of leadership and inadequate participation in the organisational and economic affairs of the agricultural institutions like cooperatives, Lack of appropriate agricultural technology aimed at reducing the physical drudgery of farm women, inadequate access to credit and agricultural inputs and other services, Lack of female farm extension workers, lack of marketing facilities and opportunities, less participation in decision-making even within the household, lack of opportunities to improve socio-economic status of farm women, lack of skills and attitudes in leadership and management are some of the constraints suffered by the farm women. They are still given a raw deal.

One of the latest reports of UN FAO points out that helping the women farmers could increase agriculture output in the developing countries by as much as 2.5 per cent to 4 per cent per annum.

1.6 The Problem of Grain Drain

A report of the FAO reveals that food grains worth $ 750 billion gets wasted every year across the globe and Asian countries like China and India are the leading ones when it comes to food wastage. This amount is equivalent to GDP of Switzerland. The report says that of the total wastage 54 per cent gets wasted during production, harvesting, cleaning and storage and the rest 46 per cent gets wasted during processing and distribution. At a time when about 87 crore peoples go to the bed hungry; wasting this much of food is by no means justified.

Back home, the overall production of food grains in the country has now crossed 250 million tonnes. We had already crossed the midway point in the time frame set for achieving the UN Millennium Development Goals. But still there is the widespread prevalence of hunger and poverty in the country.

The Global Hunger Report 2014 records the hunger status of the country still in the 'serious' category. If we look at the global scenario, the Global Hunger Index score in 1990 was 20.6 for the developing world whereas 2014 GHI stands at 12.5 representing a reduction of 30 per cent. Despite progress levels of hunger remain alarming or extremely alarming in 16 countries. Countries like Mozambique (GHI 20.5), Yemen (GHI 23.4), Eriteria (GHI 33.8) and Burundi (35.6) are still in the alarming and extremely alarming category. Unfortunately in 2011-2013, 805 million peoples were chronically undernourished. Malnutrition affects one in two people on the planet. About 165 million children under the age of five suffer from stunting, while two billion people are deficient in one or more essential micronutrients, such as vitamin A, zinc, and iron.

One of the reasons behind this widespread prevalence of hunger and malnutrition is the loopholes in the Public Distribution System. A couple of years back food grains worth 580 billion got spoiled due to lack of adequate storage facilities with the Food Corporation of India. What was shocking was that thousand of quintals of wheat meant for the poor were sold at few paisa per Kg as manure for the simple reason that the water from river Ghaggar in Haryana had entered the wheat bags which were kept open. I would here like to mention here a few lines of an article on rotten food and Poverty by former CBI chief Joginder Singh that appeared in The Tribune. The lines read as 'so much is the quantity of food grains kept in the open that if each bag was stacked one upon the other, there was no need to launch a scientific expedition to put a man on the moon'. It further said that rotten food grain was so rotten that even the animals would not eat it. For last so many years leakages and diversion of food grains meant for BPL families have been reported. A study by Tata Economic Consultancy on the extent of diversion reported 36 per cent diversion in case of wheat, 31 per cent of rice and 23 per cent of sugar at the national level. The Wadhwa committee in 2001 reported that subsidy amounting to 28.000 crore meant for Delhi in fact went to the coffers of corrupt officers. The central vigilance committee constituted by Honorable Supreme Court revealed holistic collapse of PDS because of holistic corruption. All this necessitates looking for alternatives to Public Distribution System. The report of the National Sample Survey Organization (NSSO) with regard to the diversion of food grains meant for PDS is noteworthy. In 1999-2000, about one-tenth of the rice was diverted, whereas nearly half (49 per cent) of all wheat was diverted. However, the proportion of rice that is diverted has been increasing rapidly - from just 9.9 per cent in 1999-2000 to 18.2 per cent in 2001-2 and to 41.3 per cent in 2004-5. Since 2004-5, there has been a marginal decline in the percentage of rice that is being diverted. At the all India level, the leakages from the PDS increased from 24 per cent to 54 per cent. Even among the better performing southern states (for instance, Kerala) there was deterioration. Among the states Maharashtra and Karnataka have very high diversion rates (over 40 per cent). The estimated diversion ratio was around 54 per cent in 2004-05, the last year for which detailed data are available from a "thick round" of the NSSO. Tamil Nadu had the lowest diversion rate (around 7 per cent); the rate was well below the national average in the other southern States also (around 25 per cent in each case). This was in contrast to states like, Bihar, Jharkhand, Assam, and Rajasthan where the estimated diversion rates ranged between 85 and 95 per cent. These estimates, if proved correct, suggest a comprehensive breakdown of the PDS in these States at that time. The results of NSSO 63rd and 64th round revealed that things have improved, though only marginally, at the all India level. The overall diversion of grain has come down from 54 per cent in 2004-5 to 44 per cent in 2007-08. The problem of grain drain is a curse on the country's distribution system. Suitable measures need to be taken to plug the loopholes in the system. These have discussed in the Chapter Reforming Public Distribution System.

1.7 Minimum Support Prices and the Farmer's Dilemma

With a vast majority of the population being dependent upon agricultural produce as their main source of livelihood, they expect a fair price of their produce so as to start preparing for the next crops. But defying the very logic the consumers of food grains are made to dictate terms on the very producers of food grains. Often it is seen that the due to lack of necessary infrastructure and marketing support farmers get exploited at the hands of middlemen where they were and are forced to sell their produce at throw away prices. To prevent the exploitation of the farming community the government came up with the idea of Minimum Support Prices. It is the price at which government procures food grain from the farmers. Besides MSP the Central government also announces the CIP of food grains at which food grains are sold under different government schemes and allocations of quantity of food grains under Targeted Public Distribution Scheme (TPDS). The MSP is based on the recommendations of the CACP. Although MSP is announced for 24 different crops including Rice, Wheat, Bajra, Ragi, Pulses, oilseed crops etc, yet it is effective mostly for Paddy and Wheat only. There has been a huge cry over the MSP. Farmers often complained about the low MSP. The Center for Sustainable Agriculture in Andhra Pradesh calculated that cost of cultivation for Paddy in 2011-12 was rupees 1800 per quintal where as the MSP in the same year was 1,080. That is why a very low percentage of farmers sell their produce to the government agencies. They sell their produce in the open market where they get higher returns than the MSP announced by the central government. Farmers demand that the MSP for a particular crop should be fifty per cent more than the cost of cultivation of that particular crop. All agriculture inputs seed, fertilizers, plant protection chemicals and the labour have become so costly. The costs of fertilizers and seeds though are regulated by the government but the actual price the farmer pay are higher as sometimes they have to get these commodities in black. The way the rupee is falling against the dollar, it seems the things particularly the rising input costs have become irreversible; one can never hope that the price will get lowered. The fate of MSP is such that even the than Agricultural minister Sh. Sharad Pawar shoot of a letter to than Prime Minister Mr. Manmohan Singh to protest against the group of ministers decision not to allow the export of cotton beyond 13 million bales in the year 2012. What happened was that the prices of cotton fall below the Minimum Support Prices.

Government of India has been following an open ended policy in case of grain procurement as there is no ceiling on the amount of procurement. The FCI procures whatever is offered to it. While rice and wheat are the two major crops where the government interventions are more pronounced, for other crops procurement is carried out when the market prices of the crops fall below the MSP. Farmers feel that the periodical rise in MSP is too low to compensate for the rising cost of agricultural inputs. Contrary to this Economist S. S. Bhalla holds the view that Indian farmers receive the highest price for Paddy globally. High MSP increase the food subsidy bill and thus the inflation ultimately making the commodities inaccessible for the poor. MSP were basically set up as a floor prices below which market price cannot fell. It has also been reported that it has resulted in farmers in states like Punjab and Haryana directing more land under the cultivation of these two crops severely reducing the prospects of diversification. Rather than this the farmers should be encouraged to shift towards diversification and to grow crops with least use of inputs by using crop intensification techniques.

1.8 Agriculture Credit

The World Bank (1975) in its sector policy paper has aptly reiterated 'Credit is often a key element in the modernization of agriculture'. Not only can credit remove financial constraint but it also accelerates adoption of new technology (Patel, 2103). Credit is also one of the vital inputs in agriculture. The different operations as well as different inputs in agriculture require money and as such availability of credit at the right time and in right quantity to a very great extent determines the agricultural production. The relevance of timely agricultural credit has also been highlighted by our President Sh. Pranav Mukherjee and the than Finance minister who had said that, 'given the importance of credit to agriculture sector, it has been our endaveour to ensure timely availability of credit in adequate measure at an affordable cost to farmers'. The flow of agricultural credit witnessed a rapid increase after the first round of bank nationalization, but the limited access of small and marginal farmers to institutional credit continues to be a matter of concern. There is no dearth of agencies with the responsibility of providing credit to the farmers but the reality is that the farmers are still being outside the ambit of institutional credit. The Banks are still reluctant to advance loans to the farming community. The cumbersome process of obtaining loans is also another obstacle in the way of farmers getting the loans. As compared to the institutional sources many of the farmers still go to landlords to obtain loans for agricultural purposes. These money lenders charge huge rate of interest from these farmers ultimately the farmer finds himself trapped and is left with no option except to end his life. The 59th round (January-December, 2003) report of NSSO on situational assessment of farm indebtness in the country estimated that the 60.4 per cent of the rural households were farmer households and of them 48.6 per cent were indebted. Andhra Pradesh ranked first in indebtness (82 per cent), followed by Tamil Nadu (74.5 per cent), Punjab (65.4 per cent), Kerala (64.4 per cent), Karnataka (61.6 per cent), and Maharashtra (54.8 per cent). The survey also found that of every 100 indebted households, 29 have taken from professional money lenders. Again Andhra Pradesh took the lead with 57 out of 100 indebted households having taken credit from professional money lenders.

According to AIDIS, the share of total debt of cultivar-households taken from formal sources fell from 64 per cent in 1992 to 57 per cent in 2003. In the same period the share of total debt taken from money lenders doubled from 10.5 per cent to 19.6 per cent (Khan, M. J. 2012). Money lenders still are the bane of Indian agriculture. The easy access, lesser formalities and no legalities make these money lenders the favorite of the farming community. The Rural Credit Survey Report that shows contribution of different credit giving agencies and the percentage proportion of borrowing from each agency to the total borrowings of cultivators is presence below in Table 3.

Table 3: Relative Proportion of Borrowing from each Agency to Total Borrowings of Cultivators

Sl.No.	*Credit Agency*	*Proportion of Borrowing from each Agency to Total Borrowings of Cultivators*
1.	Government	3.3
2.	Cooperatives	3.1
3.	Relatives	14.2
4.	Landlords	1.5
5.	Agriculturist money lenders	24.9
5.	Professional money lenders	44.4
6.	Traders and Commission agents	5.5
7.	Commercial Banks	0.9
8.	Others	1.8

Source: The Rural Credit Survey Report.

Presently agricultural credit is disbursed through commercial Banks, Regional Rural Banks and Cooperatives with Commercial Banks accounting for 70.6 per cent of all the rural credit advancement. The Cooperative Credit Societies Act was enacted in 1904 to combat rural indebtness and to provide a legal and formal institutional status to credit societies. The cooperative system was unable to provide adequate support to the needy farmers and rural entrepreneurs as the demand for credit for agricultural inputs, seeds and fertilizers and other items grew many times. At the grass-root level of the three tier cooperative credit delivery system in India are the Primary Agricultural Cooperative Societies (PACS). These are entrusted with the task of providing credit to poor and weaker sections of the society. As on March 31, 2012, 7.27 lakh villages in India were covered with as many as 93,423 cooperative credit societies (Table 4). But these institutions at the lowest level are on the decline. The non performing assets have increased. These are now depending heavily on refinancing from other financial institutions. The weak possibility of internal generation of resources has also put a question mark on the sustainability of these bodies.

Table 4: Vital Statistics about PACS

Sl.No.	Indicators	Total No.
1.	No. of PACS (including no profit no loss PACs also)	93,413
2.	No. of Villages	7,27,911
3.	Village/PAC ratio	7.8:1
4.	No. of Profit making PACS	44,554
5.	No. of Loss making PACS	38,065
6.	Per cent profit making PACS to total	47.69
7.	Per cent loss making PACS to total	40.74

Source: Tripathy, 2013

Now, thrust is given to institutional credit and it has resulted in an increase of farm credit from 85,000 crore about seven years back to more than 5 lakh crore this year (Basu, P. K. 2013). Now farm loans are available at 7 per cent per year and crop loans are available at 4 per cent per year subject to a limit of rupees three lakh. The scheme of KCC has also been started by the government. KCC is a provision for providing loans to meet the short time credit requirements of the farmers. As on March 31, 2008 714.68 lakh number of KCC were issued of which cooperative Banks accounted for 49 per cent, commercial Banks (37 per cent) and Regional Rural Banks (14 per cent). Owing to the simplicity of the scheme farmers prefer KCC for credit purposes. As per the ICAR estimates to meet the food requirements of our growing populations it is imperative that our rice and cereal production should grow by 30 per cent, pulses by 140 per cent and oilseeds by 243 per cent by 2020. As such the credit need of the farming community needs to be looked in promptly.

1.9 Agricultural Subsidies

Subsidy has been one of the contentious issues in Indian economy. Sharma and Thaker have described subsidies as a government intervention in agriculture to achieve a wide range of economic and social objectives. The reasons of course are varied; from being self sufficiency to employment generation, supporting small farmers for adopting modern technology and inputs, reduce price instability and improve income of famers by increasing yields. Subsidies refer to a transfer of resources by the government to the buyer or seller of a good or service that has the effect of reducing the price paid by the sellers or reducing the cost of production of the good or service (Bagchi, 2013). Subsidies on food, petroleum and fertilizer make up for the bulk of total subsidies in India. Subsidies suffer from typical exclusion as well as inclusion error. While the exclusion error is due to the fact that a large number of deserving farmers do not get the benefit of subsidies, the inclusion error is because a large number of deserving farmers do not get the benefit of the subsidies. Should these be retained or they must be made to go. This is debatable and there is a serious debate going on among the country's top policy makers, planners and intellectuals. The oil subsidy bill is expected to be rupees 1, 50, 000 crore in financial year 2013-14. This is unsustainable and driving force behind India's current account deficit of 4.8 per cent of GDP. The then finance Minister Mr. P. Chidambaram said that for every one rupee of the benefit to the poor through subsidies government need to spend rupees three. This amount can be doubled by replacing subsidies with cash transfers. Food subsidy costs India $23 billion per annum.

Regarding subsidies there are different schools of thoughts. While one school of thought says subsidies must go the other school says it has to be there and still another says it should be made farmer specific. Some economists opined that government spending on food subsidy raises the purchasing power of the poor and this purchasing power of the poor is likely to be spent on other local goods thus raising employment opportunities. Now subsidies are being replaced by cash transfers. The Kelkar Committee also was of the view that a gradual removal of subsidies would not only enable the government to spend more on economic growth oriented projects but would also help in attracting private investments. Going ahead the twelfth five year plan also recommended some control on the subsidies without harming the interests of farming community. Serious apprehensions are being raised about whether the subsidies particularly the fertilizer subsidy benefits the farmers or the fertilizer industry (Gulati, 1990, Gulati and Narayanan, 2003). Furthermore, it has been revealed that the benefits of fertilizer subsidy are heavily tilted in favour of large farmers growing water-intensive crops like rice, sugarcane, wheat, cotton, in a handful of states. Studies have revealed that most of the fuel subsidies in the country are enjoyed by the people in the high income groups. The agricultural subsidies are more than four times that of public investment in rural infrastructure (World Bank, 2008). Chand and Pandey also studied the impact of fertilizer subsidy on Indian agriculture. They reported that one per cent change in fertilizer price in real terms cause 0.125 per cent change in food grains production in opposite direction and if the subsidy on fertilizer is removed completely, it will result in 69 per cent increase in the cost of fertilizers and this will lead to a 9 per cent reduction in food grains production in the country (Singh and Chand, 2010). Chand and Pandey therefore argued that its abolition is not desirable for the country from food security point of view. Before arriving at any conclusion a careful analysis of the subsidy trends to interpret the consequences is necessary.

Table 5: Agriculture Subsidies (in US $) in Selected Countries (1999)

Country/Region	*Per Hectare*	*Per Farmer*
United States of America	129	21,000
European countries	832	17,000
OECD	218	11,000
India	53	66

1.9.1 Subsidy trends in the Post Liberalization Period

If we see the subsidy trends in the country, we will observe that the total subsidies (food and fertilizer) have increased from Rs. 12,158 crore in 1990-91 to Rs. 1,29,243 crore in 2008-09 representing an increase by 10.6 times. If we take the case of fertilizer subsidy alone it increased from Rs. 4389 crore in 1990-91 to Rs. 65,837 crore in 2010-11 (Table 6). As a percentage of GDP, this represents an increase from 0.85 per cent in 1990-91 to 1.52 per cent in 2008-09. The fertilizer subsidy in India as percentage of the GDP varied from 0.47 in 2002-03 to 1.52 per cent in 2008-09. While the average crop response to fertilizers was 25 kilograms of grain per kg of fertilizer during the 1960s, this fell to 8 kg by the late 1990s (Kapur 2011). During the last decade, while fertilizer consumption grew by 50 per cent, the increase in food grains production was only 11 per cent. The increase in fertilizer use has come at significant costs. While the fertilizer subsidy's fiscal burden was merely Rs 60 crore in 1976-77, it shot up to more than Rs 65,000 crore in 2010-11 (Table 6).

Table 6: Central Subsidy on all Fertilizers (in Rupees crore)

Year	*Total Subsidy*
1976-77	60
1980-81	505
1985-86	1924
1990-91	4389
1995-96	6735
2000-01	13,800
2005-06	18,460
2010-11	65,837

1.9.2 Size of Farm and Fertilizer Use

Studies shows that the share of small and marginal farmers in total operational holdings increased from 77.4 per cent in 1991-92 to a little more than eighty per cent in 2001-02. In the same period the share of large holdings declined marginally from 1.6 per cent to 1.2 per cent. Medium and large holdings (with holding size of more than 4 ha) with a share of 6.8 per cent used just over one-fourth of total fertilizer consumed in the country in 2001-02. In contrast, the small and marginal farmers, which constituted about 82 per cent of total holdings, consumed 52 per cent of total fertilizers. The share of small and marginal farmers in total operational holdings increased by 4.8 per cent between 1991-92 and 2001-02 but their share in total fertilizer use increased by over 10 per cent. However, if we compared the relative shares of different farm size groups in total operational area and fertilizer use, the scenario gets completely changed. In 2001-02, small and marginal farmers accounted for 42.6 per cent of area operated but accounted for 52 per cent of total fertilizer consumption in the country. On the other hand medium and large farmers, which accounted for over one-third of operational area, consumed 25.9 per cent of total fertilizer used in the country in 2001-02. In 2001-02, over 77 per cent of the gross cropped area was fertilized on marginal holdings while nearly 50 per cent of the area was fertilized on large farms. An inverse relationship between farm size and proportion of fertilized area to gross cropped area was witnessed during all the years. The intensity of fertilizer use was significantly higher on small and marginal farms compared to large farms. The average fertilizer consumption per hectare of gross cropped area was the highest (126.2 kg) on marginal holdings and the lowest on large farms (55.9 kg) in 2001-02. Similar trend was observed during 1991-92 and 1995-96. Moreover there has been a significant increase in fertilizer intensity on all farm size holdings during the period 1991-92 and 2001-02. However, the increase was the largest (74.8 per cent) on marginal farms (from 72.2 kg/ha in 1991-92 to 126.2 kg/ha in 2001-02), followed by small holdings (53.7 per cent) and the lowest (21.4 per cent) on large farms.

It is worth mentioning that benefits of fertilizer subsidy have spread to unirrigated areas as the share of area treated with fertilizers has increased from 41 per cent in 1996-97 to 53.5 per cent in 2001-02 on unirrigated lands. This share is substantially higher in irrigated areas (91.6 per cent in 2001-02). Likewise, the share of unirrigated areas in total fertilizer use had also increased from 26 per cent in 1996-97 to 30.7 per cent in 2001-02. Per hectare fertilizer use on unirrigated lands has increased by about 42 per cent between 1996-97 and 2001-02 (35.8 kg/ha to 50.9 kg/ha). In case of irrigated areas, intensity of fertilizer use was significantly higher compared with unirrigated area but had increased at a lower rate (13.1 per cent) between 1996-97 and 2001-02. It is quite evident from the above discussion that benefits of fertilizer subsidy are not restricted to only resource-rich areas but have spread to other areas as well. The inequity in distribution of fertilizer subsidy among states is still large but has declined over time. The share of subsidies used for the unirrigated land has increased over time. In their study Sharma, V. P and Thaker, H. have revealed that reduction in fertilizer subsidies could cause an adverse impact on farm production and incomes as farmers are certainly helped by lower input prices as compared to higher output prices (Bagchi, 2013).

The new nutrient based fertilizer subsidy policy in India has decontrolled phosphatic and potashic fertilizers and fixed the amount of subsidy based on the nutrient content in the fertilizers instead of the earlier system of product based subsidy. This policy allows the farmers to choose the right combination of fertilizers for their crop to achieve the right balance of nutrients to the soil profile. For this the farmers need to know the nutrient deficiencies in their soil and the recommended nutrient mix for prospective crops of their choice. This new subsidy policy will also motivate the farmers to get their soil tested regularly and get crop wise recommended doses of nutrients including micro and macro nutrients. The policy also offers prospective benefits from the point of view of agro environmental management. Application of nutrients based on the soil tests will not only reduce the demand for subsidized nutrients but also prevents overuse of these thereby avoiding the excessive leaching of nutrients into the ground water.

1.9.3 Crops and Subsidy

Studies reveal that the rice and wheat are the major users of fertilizer subsidy accounting for over half of the total subsidy. The total fertilizer used in India by five crops (rice, wheat, sugarcane, cotton, rapeseed mustard) account for 68 per cent. Major share is accounted for paddy (37 per cent) and wheat (24 per cent) among food crops. On an average farmers applied 126 kg/ha of NPK to rice in 2001-02 in the ratio of 4.3: 1.7: 1 and 132 kg/ha in the ratio of 24:10:1. In irrigated areas it was about 165 kg/ha for paddy and 143 kg NPK/ha for wheat (96-98 per cent).

Coarse cereals receive a small share of fertilizers subsidy. The farmers growing fertilizer intensive crops like paddy, wheat, sugarcane and cotton are the major beneficiaries of subsidy. So there is a high degree of concentration of fertilizer subsidies in terms of crops as four crops consume nearly two-third of total fertilizer subsidy. Studies clearly show that fertilizer subsidy is distributed more equitably among different farm sizes compared with crop-wise and state-wise distribution of fertilizer subsidy. Subsidies are among the most powerful instruments for manipulation or balancing the growth rate of production and trade in various sectors and regions and for an equitable distribution of income for the protection of weaker sections of society. The support and procurement prices for more agricultural production are some of the important measures, which are done to protect the interests of farmers. It is found that at national level during pre as well as post liberalization periods, the total subsidies have increased at different increasing rates and in absolute terms. In 2008-09, the total subsidies have increased by 94.38 times than that of 1980-81, whereas fertilizers subsidies twenty nine times, electricity subsidy 75.24

times and irrigation subsidy by 36.86 times in 2000-01 as compared to pre liberalization period (1980-81).

1.9.4 Agricultural Subsidies and Productivity of Crops in India

Substantial additional growth in agricultural production is needed to meet the basic necessities of large and growing population. It is also needed to generate agricultural surplus require for economic development with emphasis on employment equity. The bulk of growth in agricultural production will have to come from continuous increase in the productivity of land, yield based growth cannot sustain without removing soil fertility constraints and promote technological change. Among the various agriculture subsidies, fertilizer subsidy is the next largest food subsidy. Fertilizer subsidy is a development subsidy, which accelerate the fertilizer use and thus promote agricultural production. The absence of subsidies, the farmers will not able to purchase fertilizer on the higher price. In such a case farmers, fertilizer use for agricultural production will gradually decline. The removal of subsidy would affect the agricultural sector and economy. Subsidies are among the most powerful instrument for manipulating or balancing the growth rate of production and trade in various sectors for an equitable distribution of income for protection of weaker sections of the society. The support and procurement prices of major agricultural production are some of the important measures which are done to protect the interest of farmers and weaker sections of consumers. It is also needed to generate agricultural surplus required for economic development with emphasis on employment equity. The agricultural production increased in initial period gradually after than the fertilizer subsidies were reduced. The overall economy also gets effected. The government policy of subsidy is very well for protection of the weaker sections and marginal farmers (Halmandage, 2010).

Now, it can be concluded that the fiscal deficit of centre as well as states government has increased and subsidies given by centre government have also increased in all this period. As such, we cannot rush to conclusions and have to arrive at a consensus acceptable to all.

1.9.5 Agricultural Subsidies and the Food Security Act

The government of India has now enacted the food security act and the food subsidies are surely to increase. The programme when implemented will be the largest in the world and the government will have to spend rupees 1.3 lakh crore annually on supply of about 62 million tonnes of rice, wheat and coarse cereals to 67 per cent of the population. Now let us look at the subsidy portion in the right to food law. Taking today's price at which the government procures food grains from the farmers, the prices of rice and wheat are rupees 13.45 and rupees 12.85 respectively. At this price see the subsidy portion; rupees 10.45 per kilogram of rice and rupees 10.84 per kilogram of wheat (Tiwari, K. N. 2013). Another cost analysis reveals that food subsidy cost of implementing is rupees 124, 502 crores for the fiscal year 2013-14. The cost is estimated to increase to rupees 1,40,192 crore and rupees 1,57,701 crore in 2014-15 and 2015-16 respectively (Mishra, P., 2013). Some subsidies should be given and some others can be withdrawn without harming the farmers. The centre government should give subsidies to states either on the basis of gross cropped area or productivity. Subsidies which have direct relationship on productivity and income like seeds, fertilizers should be given to farmers. Another option can be to put a cap on the subsidy for large and resource rich farmers. The resourceful farmers can be given subsidies to a limited extent after which they will have to pay in full. For instance on the basis of farm size, the large families can be given subsidy for a certain amount of fertilizers, chemicals diesel or petrol and other inputs for a particular season after which they will have to purchase the same item by paying the full amount. This while on the one hand will reduce the agriculture subsidy bill and on the other hand will result in judicious use of the scarce items. Subsidies should be given to those who actually need, like small and medium size category farmers. Subsidies can be withdrawn but in a phased manner. The savings due to subsidies can be than used for infrastructural development of research purposes. There is also a need to address supply side constraints. India has inadequate infrastructure *viz.* power, roads and storage structures. Mere redistribution through increase subsidies without addressing inadequate infrastructure leads to stagflation *i.e.* slow growth with high inflation.

1.9.6 The Case of Haiti

Haiti presents an excellent example of how a developing country was negatively affected by agricultural subsidies in the developed world. Haiti was at one time self-sufficient in meeting its own needs of rice. What has happened now is that Haiti does not produce enough to feed its people and 60 per cent of the food consumed in the country is imported. Haiti liberalized its economy and threw opened its market for international players by lowering the tariffs and providing other concessions. Following this, the domestically produced rice in the country was displaced by cheaper subsidized rice from the United States. The Food and Agriculture Organization describes this liberalization process as being the removal of barriers to trade and a simplification of tariffs, which lowers costs to consumers and promotes efficiency among producers. Opening up Haiti's economy granted consumers access to food at a lower cost; allowing foreign producers to compete for the Haitian market drove down the price of rice. However, for Haitian rice farmers without access to subsidies, the downward pressure on prices led to a decline in profits. Subsidies received by American rice farmers, plus increased efficiencies, made it impossible for their Haitian counterparts to compete. According to Oxfam and the International Monetary Fund, tariffs on imports fell from 50 per cent to three per cent in 1995 and the nation is currently importing 80 per cent of the rice it consumes.

Chapter 2

MAJOR ISSUES IN INDIAN AGRICULTURE

As against the three fold increase in population, we have achieved more than fourfold increase in production (Table 6). India has achieved 725, 496, 370 and 230 per cent production gains in fish, eggs, food grains and vegetables respectively in the last 60 years (Ayappan, 2012). India is also blessed to be a tropical country with the northern half under subtropical climate and the southern half under tropical climate, both being conducive for farming. Indian agriculture is unique with five agro ecosystem and 14 production systems with dry land as a major contributor (Singh R. P, 2012). India has the second largest area under cultivation, highest area under irrigation 55.8 m ha (China has 54.5 m ha under irrigation and United States has 22.4 m ha under irrigation), world's largest user of fertilizers (11 per cent of world's dosage), first in production of Pulses (Masood *et al.* 2009), second in production of cereals like Wheat (Sredhar, 2012) and second in production of vegetables next only to China (Gupta, 2012). Besides the country has the largest livestock population and is at 2nd position in terms of total cattle population in the world (Sharma and Tiwari, 2011).

Table 7: Indian Population vs. Food Grains Production

Year	*Population (million)*	*Food Grains Production (m.MT)*
1951	36.10	50.82
1961	43.92	82.01
1971	54.81	108.42
1981	68.33	129.59
1991	84.64	176.39
2001	102.87	196.81
2011	1210	241.58
2021 (Estimated)	1300	310

Source: Rao and Mishra, 2011.

While the contribution of agriculture to the Gross Domestic Product has declined to 14 per cent, the level of dependence on agriculture for livelihood remained above 50 per cent. Due to the pressure of population, the per capita availability of land has shrinked to 0.12 hectare in last 60 years. The overall growth rate of 8 per cent has remained hollow for the farming community. The farmer non farmer inequality has increased from 1:3 in 1987-88 to 1:8 now (Singh R. P, 2012). The non redressal of this gap over the years has been the main cause for widening social and economic gaps.

Agriculture in India today is plagued with several contentious issues. The major issues in Indian agriculture are as:

2.1 Declining Share of Investment in Agriculture

The percentage share of investment in agriculture and allied activities to total plan outlay has declined from 14.9 per cent in the first five year plan to 3.6 per cent in eleventh five year plan (2007-12) (Planning commission, GoI). The amount of investment we made in agriculture research, extension and education is directly related to the Total Factor Productivity (TFP). Public investment in bringing more and more area under irrigation, creating the necessary infrastructure for making farms more accessible to the markets, providing a chain of cold stores, refrigerated vans, facilities for value addition and food processing so as to reduce the post harvest losses, funds for research on plant varieties suitable for different agro climatic zones and for transferring the technology to the clientele are necessary for TFP growth. The share of Gross capital formation (GCF) of agriculture and allied sector in total GCF has hovered between 6 to 8 per cent whereas it was around 18 per cent during 1980's. This indicates that the sectors other than the agriculture are receiving more investment than agriculture resulting in growth disparities (Anonymous, 2012). The decline in the total investment particularly the public sector investment in agriculture is the main cause for declaration. It is very important to maintain a steady growth rate in TFP. As TFP increases, the cost of production decreases and prices also decrease and stabilize. Both producers and consumers share the benefits. More than half of the required increase in yield to meet the target of demand must be met from research efforts by developing location specific and low input use technology with emphasis on the regions where the current yields are below the required national average yield. All this requires increased investment.

2.2 Land Use Dynamics

Of the total land mass of 328.73 million hectares in the country, the reported area for land utilization has been 305 million hectares (Kuriakose and Iyer, 2011). This includes 141 million hectare as net sown area, 70 million hectare under forests, 26 million hectare under non agricultural use, 25 million ha fallow land, 17 million hectare barren and unculturable land, 13 million hectare culturable waste land, 10 million hectare under permanent pasture and other grazing land and 3 million hectare under miscellaneous tree crops and groves (Table 8). The net sown area in 1950-51 was 119 million hectares and it increased substantially during the 1950's and 1960's to 141 million hectares in 1970-71, Thereafter there has been virtually no addition to Net sown area till present. As observed the Net sown area at the aggregate country level has remained constant during the post liberalization period. However disaggregated analysis at the regional levels indicate that it has increased; in northeast annual rate of addition to NSA being 31,450 hectares while there has been decline in the subsector in southern eastern and western regions and the annual rate of depletion being 1,36,330; 50, 840; and 33,060 ha respectively (Barddhan and Tewari, 2010). It seems that reclamation and development of cultivable wastes is adding to the cultivable area on the one hand and the addition to the fallow land is depleting the cultivated area thereby nullifying the efforts going behind wasteland reclamation and development. The fact that net sown area has remained constant or declined during the period further corroborates the point. We have to strike a balance in use of land.

Table 8: Land Use Dynamics in India in Million Hectares (m ha)

Total geographical area	328 m ha
Net sown area	141 m ha
Area under forest	70 m ha
Area under non agricultural use	26 m ha
Fallow land	25 m ha
Barren and Unculturable land	17 m ha
Culturable waste land	13 m ha
Permanent pastures and other grazing land	10 m ha
Miscellaneous tree crops and grooves	3 m ha

Source: State of Indian Agriculture, 2011-12.

2.3 Declining Size of Operational Holdings

The average size of operational land holdings has decreased progressively from 2.28 ha in 1970-71 to 1.55 ha in 1990-91 to 1.23 ha in 2005-06. More than eighty per cent of the holdings are marginal and small having size of less than 2 hectares (Table 9). However recent studies have revealed that there are about 115 million operational holdings in the country and more than 90 per cent of these are marginal and small land holdings (Prasad, 2011).

Table 9: Percentage of different Size of Holdings as per Agriculture Census 2005-06

Size of Holdings	*Percentage*
Marginal (< 1 ha)	64.80
Small (1-2 ha)	18.00
Medium (>2 to < 10 ha)	16.00
Large (10 ha and above)	>1.00

Source: State of Indian agriculture, 2011-12.

2.4 The Low Yields

Low yields per unit of area across almost all crops have become a regular feature of the Indian agriculture (Table 10). Though India accounted for more than 20 per cent of global Paddy acreages the estimated yield per hectare is less than the global average. Similarly, in wheat while India accounted for 12 per cent of the global production its yield is not impressive (Tuteja, 2007).

2.5 Low Level of Farm Mechanization

Farm mechanization in India has been a typical case of Tractorisation rather than mechanization. At present in India, tractors are being used for tillage of 22.78 per cent of total area and sowing 21.30 per cent of total area. Owing to more than eighty per cent of small and marginal farms there should have been more mechanization by providing the equipments for tillage, sowing, irrigation, plant protection and threshing. Emperical evidence confirms a strong relationship between farm mechanization and agricultural productivity. This is because farm mechanization saves time and labour ultimately reducing the total cost involved in various operations. The percentage level of mechanization in different crops and different operations is depicted in Table 11.

2.6 Rainfed Agriculture

Of the net cultivated area of 141 million hectares in India, 57 million hectares (40.4 per cent) is irrigated and about 84 million hectares (59.6 per cent) is rainfed (Kalkoti, 2013). These area were largely bye passed by the green revolution and represent low input farming characterized by low fertility of soil leading to low productivity and low profitability, less water retention capacity of the soils, crop failures and land degradation and expected to be hit hard by the Climate change. Until we make rainfed areas the cradle of second green revolution; these will continue to remain underinvested undermining the full potential of agricultural sector.

2.7 Food Processing

Food processing in India is still in the nascent stage as only 2 per cent of the food is processed. This is despite the fact that the food processing industry in the country is the largest and ranked fifth in terms of production, consumption, export and expected growth. Dairy sector accounts for 37

Table 10: Area, Production and Yield of different Crops in India (2011-12)

Sl.No.	*Crop*	*Area (000 ha)*	*Production (000 tonnes)*	*Yield (q/ha)*
1.	Wheat	29,865	94,882	31.8
2.	Rice	44,006	1,05,311	23.9
3.	Maize	8,782	21,759	24.8
4.	Jowar	6,245	6,006	9.6
5.	Bajra	8,777	10,276	11.7
6.	Barley	643	1,619	25.2

Source: Ministry of Agriculture; Govt. of India.

per cent of the total food processed; out of that just 15 per cent is processed in the organized sector (Table 12).

Table 11: Level of Mechanization of different Farm Operations in Indian Agriculture

Operation	*Percentage Level of Mechanization*
Tillage	40.2
Tractor	15.6
Animal	24.7
Sowing with drills and planters	28.9
Tractors	8.3
Animals	20.6
Plant protection	34.2
Irrigation	37
Threshers	
Wheat	47.8
Paddy and others	4.4
Harvesting	
Reapers	0.56
Combines	0.37

Source: Proceedings of 20th National Convention of Agricultural Engineers held at PAU, Ludhiana on Jan19-20, 2007.

Table 12: Level of Food Processing in India

Segments	*Processing in the Organized Sector (per cent)*	*Processing in the Unorganized Sector (per cent)*	*Total Food Processed (per cent)*
Fruits and Vegetables	1.2	0.5	1.7
Dairy Products	15	22	37
Meat	21	–	21
Poultry	6	–	6
Marine fishes	1.7	9	10.7
Shrimps	0.4	1	1.4

Source: Ministry of Food Processing, GoI.

2.8 Wastage in different Crops

Wastage in different crops is also a major issue globally as well as in Indian agriculture. A saving of 15 per cent in food wastage is good enough to feed 25 million hungry Americans. According to the Alliance of Liberals and Democrats in Europe almost 90 million tonnes of food gets wasted every year. In a region where 79 million people live below the poverty line and 16 million depend on food aid from charities, the entire wastage if saved could leave a lot for export to hungry people (Sharma, D. 2012). A recent study by Central institute of Post Harvest Engineering and Technology (CIPHET), Ludhiana revealed that the wastage varies from 0.8 per cent in milk to 18 per cent in fruits and vegetables (Table 13). Wastage in fruits varies between 5.8 (in Sapota) to a maximum of 18 per cent (for Guava). In vegetables, cauliflower has the minimum waste percentage at 6.8 per cent while tomato has the maximum of 12.4 per cent loss.

Wastage for other items was much lower. For crops, it was (3.9 to 6 per cent), cereals (4.3 to 6.1 per cent), pulses (4.3-6.1 per cent), oilseeds (6 per cent), meat (2.3 per cent), fish (2.9 per cent) and poultry (3.7 per cent). Post harvest losses of major agriculture produce including fruits and vegetables at the national level were estimated to be the tune of about rupees 44,000 crore (Tiwari, R. 2012).

Table 13: Per cent Wastage in Various Crops

Crops	*Cumulative Waste Percentage*
Cereals	3.9-6
Pulses	4.3-6.1
Oilseeds	6.0
Fruits and Vegetables	5.8-18
Milk	0.8
Fisheries	2.9
Meat	2.3
Poultry	3.7

Source: CIPHET, Ludhiana.

2.9 Grain Drain

One of the reasons behind this widespread prevalence of hunger and malnutrition is the loopholes in the Public Distribution System. A few years back food grains worth 580 billion got spoiled due to lack of adequate storage facilities with the Food Corporation of India. What was shocking was that thousand of quintal of wheat meant for the poor was sold at few paisa per Kg as manure for the reason that the water from river Ghaggar in Haryana had entered the wheat bags which were kept open. For last so many years leakages and diversion of food grains meant for BPL families have been reported. The report of the National Sample Survey Organization (NSSO) with regard to the diversion of food grains meant for PDS is noteworthy. In 1999-2000, about one-tenth of the rice was diverted, whereas nearly half (49 per cent) of all wheat was diverted. The proportion of rice that is diverted has been increasing rapidly from just 9.9 per cent in 1999-2000 to 18.2 per cent in 2001-2 and to 41.3 per cent in 2004-5 (Kumar, P. 2012). A study by Tata Economic Consultancy on the extent of diversion reported 36 per cent diversion in case of wheat, 31 per cent of rice and 23 per cent of sugar at the national level. The Wadhwa committee in 2001 reported that subsidy amounting to 280 billion went to the coffers of corrupt officers. The central vigilance committee constituted by Honorable Supreme Court revealed holistic collapse of PDS because of holistic corruption. The issue has been dealt in separately under chapter of this book.

Chapter 3
THE HANDICAPPED ZONE: RAINFED AGRICULTURE

The pathetic condition and the handicap of the rainfed areas can be gauzed from the estimates that one hectare of land under irrigated crops generate 600 man days of employment in a year while one hectare of dry land generate hardly 200 man days of labour in a year (Mahalingam, N, 2012). Still, It would not be wrong to say that the crux of the country's food security lies in this handicapped zone. Without giving due consideration to it, it would be ridiculous to talk of food security. Rainfed agriculture contributes in a big way both in terms of area and production to the economy at national as well as global level. These dry lands suffer from pervasive poverty. Although the absolute poverty rate in Asia's dry lands (34 per cent) is less than in sub-saharan Africa (47 per cent), twice as many absolute poor inhabit Asia (185 million) than in Africa (95 million). Walker in 2010 by using the data from World Bank (2009) revealed that 12 out of 19 of the deepest poverty trap areas in sub-saharan Africa were in dry lands. Dry land in Asia outstrips Africa in childhood malnutrition also. Rainfed agriculture is predominantly in arid, semi arid and sub humid region of the country. About 93 per cent of area in Sub Saharan African region, 87 per cent in Latin America, 67 per cent in Near East and Eastern Africa, 65 per cent in East Asia and 58 per cent in South Asia is rainfed. As such the contribution of rainfed agriculture in the global economy cannot be underestimated. The geographical and demographic dividend warrants a continued priority to rainfed agriculture. The impending effect of climate change will further add the dimensions of urgency to rainfed agriculture. India has a geographical area of 328.73 million hectare and about 60 per cent is rainfed. Almost every state in India has rainfed area but three major rainfed zones have been recognized. The first one is the Indo-gangetic Plains of North India comprising areas of Rajasthan, Punjab, Haryana, North West Madhya Pradesh and is characterized by light and heavy loamy soils. The second zone comprises of Tropical plateau of Peninsular India covering states of Maharashtra, Karnataka, and Andhra Pradesh. About 40 per cent of land of this zone is not fit for cultivation. The third zone is the Plateau of granite formation characterized by red and black cotton soils deficient in Nitrogen and Phosphorous. Rainfed areas are home to 40 per cent of world population; contribute 42 per cent of total food grains production with 90 per cent of sorghum, millets, groundnut, 75 per cent of pulses, 80 per cent of oilseeds and 65 per cent of cotton coming from the rainfed areas. Population now is growing at the rate of 1.6 per cent and going by the rate of population growth we need to produce 320 million tonnes of food grains by 2030. Even if full irrigation potential is realized, we will be able to irrigate only 178 m ha of land. Therefore we need to have a comprehensive policy for these areas. The post independence era has seen a phenomenal increase in the agriculture production in this region. The production of wheat and cotton has increased by 11 times, rice by 4 times and oilseeds by 5 times.

The rainfed areas still cry for development being bye passed by the Green revolution of sixties and the technological interventions thereafter. Peoples still practice traditional ways of cultivation and have no access to modern technology. The farmers here are resource poor but rich in Indigenous traditional knowledge. The yield of food grains in these areas is comparatively low (0.7 to 0.8 tons/ha) as compared to the irrigated areas which vary from 1-2 tons/ha as compared to maximum obtainable yield of 4 tons/hectare (Charyulu *et al.*, 2007). The fertilizer use here is three times less as compared to the irrigated areas. The area is also characterized by acute fodder shortage and poor livestock productivity.

The important characteristics of rainfed areas as compared to rainfed areas have been depicted in the Table 14.

Table 14: Important Characteristics of Predominantly Rainfed and Irrigated Areas

Characteristics	Rainfed	Irrigated
Population density (peoples/square km)	163	297
Proportion of small farms (per cent)	52	76
Poverty ratio; head count (per cent)	37	33
Land productivity (in rupees/ha)	5,716	8,017
Labour productivity (in rupees/ha)	6,842	9,830
Food grains consumption (kg/capita/annum)	260	471
Bank credit (in rupees/ha)	1,050	1,650

Source: www.iwmri.org.

Global analysis of over 100 agricultural developmental projects found that yield levels in projects focused on improving rainfed agriculture has raised on an average by 100 per cent, while the comparable achievement in irrigated project was a yield increase of only 10 per cent. Under rainfed farming operating at a lower yield level every new investment results in relatively higher and more equitable yield response. The "Everything Everywhere" approach of taking up all major interventions uniformly across all regions of the country has not paid much dividend. The specific needs of rainfed farming besides their characterization are of paramount importance. Keeping in view the importance of rainfed agriculture and the actual yield potential of these areas broad strategies need to be devised and policies have to be framed at the micro level along with proper implementation. These strategies include:

3.1 Resource Conservation Technologies

Rainfed areas suffer from bio-physical and socio economic constraints affecting the productivity of crops and livestock. In view of the growing demand for food grains in the country, there is an urgent need to increase the productivity of rainfed areas from their current level. Besides it is also necessary to maintain their fertility levels by conserving whatever resources are left with them and to adopt technologies that prevent resource degradation. The quality of natural resources in the rainfed regions is gradually getting depleted due to over exploitation. Rainfed areas need resource conservation technologies Resource conservation technologies such as zero tillage help in minimum soil disturbance by adopting no-tillage and minimum traffic for agricultural operations. The left over crop residues on the soil surface help to maintain the soil in good health and minimize the adverse environmental effects. Integrated pest management, seeks use of pesticides when other options are ineffective. Integrated nutrient management lays emphasis on the balance use of chemical nutrients through organic sources such as FYM, biofertilizers and green manuring. Agroforestry, which offer alternate land use systems incorporate trees having multiple uses into different cropping systems thereby provide a supplementary effect to the crops. Water harvesting in rainfed areas needs to be taken on a large scale. Through water harvesting formerly abandoned and degraded lands can be cultivated, and additional crops can be grown on small patches of land owing to better rainwater retention. Farmers need to be made aware of the resource conserving technologies like Zero tillage, line sowing, system of crop intensifications, the drip and the sprinklers and the various integrated techniques

In a study conducted over an area of 440 ha from 1998 to 2000, results revealed that wheat yields in zero-till fields were invariably higher by 3 to 5 per cent compared to planting in conventionally tilled fields. This increase was attributed to timely planting of wheat when zero-till was used. Another benefit was the reduced cultivation costs to the tune of Rs 1500 to 2250 per ha that was the result of reduced costs of diesel, labour and use of plant protection chemicals.

3.2 Diversification with High Value Crops

The same cropping pattern year after year has led to the deterioration of soil health in these areas. Individual farm families have to be targeted. Diversification can involve suitable fruit trees, medicinal plants, allied enterprises like Goatry, sericulture, Apiculture, Fisheries etc. This will ensure their survival even if the crop failure occurs due to drought like situation. It will also result in the increase in number of days of employment for the farm families

3.3 Modification of Agronomic Approaches

Agronomic approaches need modification to conserve soil and moisture to achieve maximum production. Bunding should be done across the slope land should be leveled with deep summer ploughing results in deep penetration of roots into the soil. Proper tillage operations, timely sowing of seeds for lessening the weed infestation, seed treatment with suitable fungicide, seed spacing and the seed and fertilizer placement all need to be scientifically done to get higher yields. Usually the seed should be placed at a depth of 5 cm and fertilizer at a depth of 7.5 cm for better germination. Organic matter at the rate of 15-20 tonnes per hectare is beneficial. Fertilizer should be applied as a foliar spray rather than being broadcasted.

3.4 Suitable Varieties for Rainfed Areas

One of the main reasons for the low productivity of the rainfed areas is the low seed replacement ratio of these areas. While at the national level it is 25 per cent, in these areas it is yet to cross the 10 per cent mark. Therefore more research efforts are needed for release of varieties suitable for these areas as well as wide print and media publicity including demonstrations and campaigns for creating awareness among the peoples regarding the varieties. The adoption rates of high yielding varieties in rainfed areas need to catch up with that of irrigated areas. Introduction of hybrids in the crops can enhance the yield by 10 per cent per annum. In case of rice increasing the use of hybrids from present level of 3 per cent to 25 per cent can contribute additional 25 million tonnes of rice.

Indian Council of Agricultural Research has divided the country into 13 major and 127 micro level agro-climatic zones. What is needed is to establish a research and a capacity building center in each of these agro climatic zones for enabling farm families to meet the challenges of abnormal monsoons. Each one of the stations should be equipped with a meteorological station.

At the same time research on harvesting and use of rainwater has to be taken up on priority basis. Watershed development programmes have to be managed more efficiently and effectively by identifying cost effective interventions. Rooftop rain water harvesting can be a suitable option for meeting the water requirements in the rainfed areas for domestic use. Use of solar and wind power for lifting of water and conveyance is also a good option. As most of the works in Mahatma Gandhi National rural Employment Guarantee act (MGNREGA) are related to soil and water conservation, the scheme can be very useful for drought proofing in these areas. The inter basin transfer of water from water surplus basins to water deficit one can bring 35 m ha of additional land under irrigation. The rainfed areas can be exploited for the cultivation of Medicinal plants which forms an important area in the international agribusiness with an estimated growth rate of 5-10 per cent. The trade in herbal dyes, drugs and cosmetics is now to the tune of billion dollars annually. Organic products are now finding large consumer markets in India as well as abroad. Rainfed areas can be utilized for the production of organic products for urban consumers. These areas have great scope and should be tapped by corporate and big business houses by suitable investment in these areas.

Rural peoples still consist of 86 per cent small farmers, 70 per cent illiterate, 40 per cent malnourished 90 per cent devoid of any credit facility. Farmers need short term credit to carry on their agricultural operations. The economic institutions like microfinance, self help groups, and Kissan credit cards can be effectively used to promote rural enterprise by value addition, food processing resulting in more employment opportunities. The social institutions like Community property resources (CPR) can be effectively used to tackle the problem of fragmentation. Collective farming can increase profitability. Similarly, water use associations are helpful for judicious and wise use of water which is a scarce commodity in these areas. The socio-political institutions like Panchayati Raj institutions can plan for themselves according to their needs leading to their social inclusion and finally empowerment. There are so many watershed projects being run successfully by the community participation. The Sukhomajri in Haryana and Ralegoan Sindhi project in Maharashtra have improved socio-economic conditions considerable in relatively short time. All this have been attained in a short time due to community participation and equitable distribution of benefits. Who can forget the name of Sh. Rajinder Singh of Tarun Bharat Sangh in Rajasthan who made dead river alive through successful implementation of water shed concept which won him Roman Magsaysay.

Dry lands have all the potential to emerge as market oriented commercially viable and ecologically sustainable means of producing food, fibre and raw materials to benefit the farmers. What is needed is a multi pronged strategy that ensures higher inflow of institutional credit to agriculture. To put in the words of our Honorable President, "Unlike we make rainfed areas the cradle of second green revolution; these will continue to remain underinvested undermining the full potential of agricultural sector".

Chapter 4
THE HELPLESS 2000 PLUS

A survey by National Sample Survey Organization (2005) revealed that 41 per cent of farmers want to leave agriculture if any other option was available. Even in agriculturally progressive state like Punjab 37 per cent of farmers wanted to quit agriculture. Definitely the percentage must have risen high now. Further 95 per cent of farming community has no access to microfinance and insurance. 56 per cent still borrow from informal sources and 70 per cent has no deposit account in Banks. Crop insurance also covers only 4-6 per cent of farmers. Youths are not interested in agriculture. This is because agriculture is not economically rewarding and intellectually stimulating. A December 2012 report of the Institute of Applied Manpower Research (IAMR) a part of the planning commission said that on an average 2,035 farmers are losing main cultivators status every single day for the last 20 years. Census 2011 also shows that we now have 95.8 million cultivators for whom farming is their main occupation and this number is down from what was 103 million in 2001 and 110 million in 1991 (Table 14). Between 1981 and 1991 the number of cultivators (main workers) actually went up from 92 million to 110 million. The huge decline comes after post 1991.

The youth of today is no more interested in agriculture and the reason obviously is because the agriculture is no more remunerative. Agriculture is now associated with dropouts and uneducated. Moreover what is alarming is that majority of farming community want to quit this occupation.

Table 15: Number of Cultivators and Labourers

Manpower/Year	1981	1991	2001	2011
Cultivators	92	110	103	95.8
Labourers	55.4	74.5	63.4	86.1
Total agricultural workers	148.0	185.2	167.1	182.0

Table 16: Agricultural Production and Workforce

Year	Food Grain Production	Per Capita Food Grain Availability	Agricultural Workers (millions)
1950-51	51	395	97
1960-61	82	469	131
1970-71	108	455	126
1980-81	130	410	148
1990-91	176	473	185
1999-01	209	470	167

India has the largest youth population in the world that is poised to increase further in the coming decade. Nearly 70 per cent of India's population is below the age of 35 years making India the youngest nation in the world and interestingly 70 per cent of them live in rural areas. According to 2011 Census, the youth population in the country including adolescents is around 550 million. In 2020, the average Indian will be only 29-year-old, whereas in China and the United States of America the average age is estimated to be 37 years. We may utilize this demographic dividend for taking Indian agriculture to new heights by channelizing the creative energies of the youth through development of skills, knowledge and attitudes. Realizing the potential of youth, the United Nations declared 2011 as the 'International Year of Youth' in which the issue of making farming attractive to youths was deliberated vigorously. The role of youth in agriculture has been discussed at different foray. The second Global Conference on 'Agricultural Research for Development' in Uruguay also highlighted the need to bring forward youth in developing agriculture in a sustainable mode. In the Farmer's Forum Global Meeting (2012) a special session was devoted on 'Youth in Agriculture'. It recommended creation of a 'new rural reality' based on a positive image of farming as a dynamic business by which youth can become entrepreneurs. The meeting came out with the recommendation that the employment opportunities must be a blend of both on-farm and non-farm activities along the agricultural value chain.

The Government of India started the Agri-clinics and Agri-business centers (ACABC) scheme in April 2002 to create self employment opportunities for the unemployed agricultural graduates and to retain the youth in their ancestral profession. With more emphasis on diversification of agriculture to make it more profitable, extension services also need to be augmented. ACABC's provide package of input facilities, consultancy and other services to strengthen extension services and also provide employment opportunities for technically trained manpower. The purpose of this scheme is to channelize the energy of youth available in the form of unemployed agricultural graduates for providing extension services to the farming community and secondly making the agricultural graduates job providers instead of job seekers by setting their own ventures.

Public-private partnerships for example, through the agri clinic and agribusiness center (ACABC) scheme is one aspect that could be strengthened and encouraged. The ACABC program provides an integrated service to the farmer, with diagnostic facilities combined with input and equipment sales.

4.1 Attracting and Retaining Youth in Agriculture (ARYA)

Besides the RAWE which provides an opportunity to the young agricultural graduates to have a first hand and knowledge of the actual agricultural situation in the fields, the ICAR has also supported the establishment of experiential learning units in over 50 universities. The Student 'Rural Entrepreneurship and Awareness Development Yojana' (READY) programme envisaged in the XII Five-Year Plan aims at entrepreneurship development among the youth. The basic aim is to make the students READY with the grass-root level experience and entrepreneurship skills by combining together RAWE and experiential learning courses. The vast network of agricultural universities and colleges can play a leading role in cultivating self-confidence and capabilities in the students required for taking up agriculture as a profession. The XII Five-Year Plan also has proposed to initiate a programme 'Attracting and Retaining Youth in Agriculture' (ARYA). ARYA aims at analyzing the current policy environment and identifying supporting policies that can check the rate of migration of youth from rural areas. It will identify such mechanisms and models that would encourage the youth to avail the quantum of opportunities in allied sectors. It is expected that the youth educated in agriculture and allied enterprises will be able to earn a dignified livelihood from farming and other related pursuits.

Social media can be the route through which the youth can be linked to agriculture. The mobile phones have now penetrated almost every nook and corner of the country. They can be of immense importance for the rural youth in terms of providing information to the youth regarding the crops and the market prices. Farming is rarely portrayed in the media as a young person's game and can be seen as outdated, unprofitable and hard work. Greater awareness of the benefits of agriculture as a career needs to be built amongst young people, in particular opportunities for greater market engagement, innovation and farming as a business. ICT can be used to train and impart the necessary skills to equip them with decision making and proper planning to those who are unable to attend institutes of higher education. Such technologies can also reduce the costs of business transactions, increasing agriculture's profitability. Young peoples' should be given representation in policy making at different levels. Agriculture as a subject should be included in the school curriculum. At the same time the credit institutions also need to devise ways for soft loans to the youth. Agriculture has to be made more productive to make agriculture more profitable.

4.2 Creating Agripreneurs

Today our farmers are no more interested in agriculture mainly because of the low profitability in this sector. There is an immediate need to augment the income of farming community by some agri based industries. About 68.9 per cent of the population in the country lives in 6.40 lakh villages. It has also been reported that 66.2 per cent of the rural males and 81.6 per cent of the rural females are engaged in agriculture as cultivators or labourers (Gautam, H.R., 2014). As such establishing agri based industries in rural locales can create employment potential for these households. Agri based industries offer opportunities for establishing autonomous income generating units and thus becoming job providers rather than job seekers. Agriculture offers varied ways for promoting rural industries that besides operating at the micro level can also serve as a feeder for the macro industries that operate at a much larger scale. It is here also worthwhile to mention that agro industries vary from those operated at the village level by individual farmers to small scale to those operating at a larger scale involving high investments. While the village industries are owned and run by rural households with very little capital investment and a high level of manual labour like the Pickle or the Papad making, the small scale industries are characterized by medium investment and semi-automation like the edible oils rice and wheat mills. The large scale industries are characterized by large investments and a high level of automation. The three segments have come up mainly based on their ability to bring in capital and capacity to market products.

The small scale industries those generally associated with agriculture are very important for a developing country like India where there is scarcity of capital but abundance of labour. The potential of small scale industries in providing employment can be gauged from the fact that they generate more number of employment opportunities per unit of capital invested. These use labour intensive techniques. For every one lakh of fixed investments, these provide employment to 26 persons as against 4 persons in the large sectors. Agro industries although considered to be an extended arm of agriculture, yet have not received attention at par with the agriculture sector. Agro industries help in processing agricultural products such as field crops, livestock and fisheries products and thereby converting them to edible and other usable forms. They produce both edible and non-edible things. However, edible products otherwise known as processed foods form a predominant segment. Take the case of sugar industry; one of the most important industries among the various agro based industries. It is a means of livelihood for approximately 2.5 crore of peoples in the rural areas. Almost rupees 200 crore of revenue is collected from the sugar industry alone.

The Food Processing sector in India also provides enormous opportunities for job opportunities and income generation. In the country only about two per cent of the food is processed. This is very less when compared to developed countries where more than fifty per cent of the produce is processed. No doubt the country has made tremendous strides in the last 20 years in production and processing of milk and milk products. But the fact remains that only 15 per cent of all the milk produced is processed. If one would spend a few hours in the food section of the Wal-Mart departmental store in a U.S. city, one would understand the depth and width of the market for processed foods. Most of the foods on the shelves are imported from Latin American and European countries. The position is the same in Singapore, London or New York. In India the highest processing is in meat products where 21 per cent of the meat products are processed. In poultry the percentage of processing is a meager six per cent. Small scale industries require less capital and provide quick returns on investment. These use local resources. These does not requires imports of machinery or raw material besides playing a complimentary role that is feeding large scale industries. These are best suited for customized production *i.e.* designing the product as per the tastes and preferences and needs of individual customers provide part time or whole time work in rural and semi urban areas.

A study by McKinsey reiterates the importance of the food sector in India. It indicates that food in India has an economic multiplier of 2-2.5. That is for every rupee of revenue from food, the economy at large gets Rs. 2-2.50. With a huge production base, India can easily become one of the leading food suppliers to the world while at the same time serving the vast growing domestic market of over a billion people. An average Indian spends around 53 per cent of his/her income on food. The upper middle class consumers for value added products are estimated to be 300 million. The large market size, the changing life styles and the increasing health consciousness all create incredible market opportunities for food producers, the processors, the technologists and service providers in this sector. The vision 2015 document states that the FPI envisages to increase processing of perishables from six to twenty per cent, value addition from 20 per cent to 35 per cent and to increase the share of global food trade from 1.5 per cent to 3.0 per cent. What is needed is the right post harvest practices such as good processing techniques, and proper packaging, transportation and storage. All this besides creating employment opportunities for masses can play a significant role in reducing spoilage and extending shelf life. It also will helps the farmers to have higher yield, better revenues and lower the risks drastically. Consumers have access to a greater variety, better prices and new products. Ultimately the economy also gets benefitted with new business opportunities for the entrepreneurs and the work force gets employment. Therefore, it is beyond any doubt that the development of agro industries can help stabilize and make agriculture more lucrative, profitable and create employment opportunities for millions both at the production and marketing stages. Agripreneurs will therefore have to be central to ensure a sustainable supply of high-quality agricultural produce. This concept can also be added in the school curricula. In one of its kind, Nestle has helped fund agricultural programmes in Latin America. Under the programmes technical and business training is provided to students alongside their normal curriculum (Nandkishore, N, 2014). This model can be replicated in Asia. Emphasis in the country could be on the continuous education of farmers and targeted technical assistance through the agricultural extension and advisory system. An "agri-preneur" would then be a progressive farmer, a rural entrepreneur and job provider.

Chapter 5
PUBLIC DISTRIBUTION SYSTEM: CAUSALITY OF MISMANAGEMENT

The Public Distribution system (PDS) in India, one of the largest social welfare programmes in the world is a system of management of food economy. The basic objective is to distribute the food grains to the identified beneficiaries at an affordable price uninterruptedly. The distribution takes place through a network of 4,62,000 fair price shops called as ration shops spread over different locations in the country. The Planning Commission estimates that 160 million families purchase commodities from these ration shops annually. The Food Corporation of India (FCI), a government owned corporation procures and maintains Public Distribution supply. After procurement the FCI ensures that the grains are stored adequately in order to prevent spoilage. Food grains are stored by adopting suitable scientific storage techniques. The principle of 'First in and First out' is followed. This is done so as to avoid long term storage of food grains. The distribution is done by the respective state governments. Though PDS is supplemental in nature but the enhanced food grains production fulfill 50 per cent of the monthly cereal requirements of the BPL families. Public Distribution System went through different transitional phases. In 1975 it was launched as Revamped PDS (RPDS) in about 1775 blocks throughout the country. It was for blocks comprising of hilly and remote inaccessible areas where substantial poor population lived and where area specific programme such as Desert Prone Area Programme were going on. In June 1997 Targeted Public Distribution system was started.

A National Sample Survey than came out with a shocking revelation. It said that 5 per cent of the total population in the country goes to bed without taking even two square miles a day. For those one crore poorest of the Poor families from among the Below Poverty Line, the Antodya Anna Yojana (AAY) was launched. The AAY had a provision of 25 Kg of wheat and rice at rupees 2 per Kg and rupees 3 per Kg respectively. This was followed by increasing the ceiling of 25 kilogram, which was enhanced to 35 kilogram in 2002. Later on 50 lakh household mostly headed by widows were included in the scheme. Further expansion resulted in inclusion of more 50 lakh households including landless labourers and marginal farmers. Another expansion in 2005-06 added 50 lakh more beneficiaries to take the total number of beneficiaries to about 2.5 crores. But despite all our efforts, hunger and malnutrition still haunt us.

Today hunger and deprivation affects million peoples in the country. India is the home for 40 per cent of the world's underweight children. The International Food Policy Research Institute (IFPRI) has put the country in the 66th rank out of 88 countries in Global Hunger Index. India ranks below all other South Asian nations with the exception of Bangladesh. What is miserable is that no state in India is in the 'low to moderate hunger index' category. India has more states under 'alarming to extremely alarming' categories with Madhya Pradesh being the worst affected. Among other reasons for prevalence of hunger and malnutrition is our Public Distribution System. There are very serious lacunas in our distribution system. A few years back food grains worth 580 billion got spoiled due to lack of adequate storage facilities with the Food Corporation of India. What was meant for the masses was sold as manure ofr a few paisas per kilogram. The reason was that water from river Ghaggar in Haryana had entered the wheat bags which were kept open. The huge diversions and leekages are the other causes that have made this public Distribution System as Public Diversion System. A series of reports have authenticated this. The Tata Economic Consultancy reported 36 per cent diversion in case of wheat, 31 per cent of rice and 23 per cent of sugar at the national level. The Wadhwa committee in 2001 went a step further. It reported that subsidy amounting to 28,000 crore meant for Delhi in fact filled the coffers of corrupt officers. A comprehensive analysis of the Indian Public Distribution System by Bharat Ramaswami (2004-05) estimated that only 10·per cent of the PDS money reached the target population, rest all were leekages. Similarly, another planning commission report in March 2008 reported that on an aggregate level, only about 42 per cent of subsidized grains issued by the central pool reach the target group.

Leekages does not occur at a particular level. It just happens at different levels. Can one imagine it starts even when food grains have not reached the designated ration shops? This has been estimated to be about 45 per cent and if 56 MMT is the official distribution figure than this leakage comes at 25 MMT *i.e.* a net value of worth rupees 50,000 crore. The other leakage is in the form of inclusive errors. The non eligible beneficiaries who do not deserve the food grains in convenience with the officials of civil supplies manage to get ration cards and become eligible for the subsidized food grains. The 2011-12 NSSO survey indicates that there were 143 million non eligible entrees which received a monthly average 4.5 kilograms of food grains. This amounts to rupees 17,500 crore (Bhalla, S.S. 2013.) Such was the worst scenario that even the Honorable Supreme Court had to intervene and the central vigilance committee constituted by the Honorable court revealed holistic collapse of PDS, because of holistic corruption. Now the bigger question is how to get rid of this mismanagement. What other alternatives can be tried. An attempt has been made in the next section.

5.1 Different Alternatives to the PDS that can be Tried

5.1.1 Food Stamps

If we go into the history of Food Stamps programme, we find that it started with the United States in the late 1930's. The basic purpose was to ensure that citizens and people legally living in the U.S. are able to feed their families. In 1930's, the Great Depression plagued the USA and hunger was one of its most severe consequences. In efforts to help the millions of Americans struggling to feed them and their families, the first Food Stamp program was created and went into effect on May 1939 in Rochester, New York. The stamps, which were orange in color, were purchased by the individuals to help them to purchase food and household items. The person would purchase food stamps to equal their usual food expenditures. The recipient could not buy alcohol, cigarettes or other non food items which may account to abuse of food stamps. For every dollar worth of orange stamps purchased, the person was given half the amount back in the form of blue stamps. This was for the purchase of specific surplus food items only. The Food stamps programme in USA has been replaced by Supplemental Nutritional Assistance Programme but the use of food stamps can also be tried in India. Under this scheme the intended beneficiaries are provide with food stamps. Food stamps of a particular value can be provide to the peoples who can than exchange these for an equivalent amount of food grains at any shop. The shopkeepers later on can get them credited into their bank accounts. Under its WIC programme, women in USA who are pregnant or have children's up to five years of age are provided with vouchers which the recipients exchange for specific food products. The vouchers being specific in nature does not give much choice to the recipients and leaves much to the control of the federal government

5.1.2 Community Grain Storage Banks

There is a huge shortfall of infrastructure in the country. The problem gets more serious when it comes to storage. Huge quantities of food grains lying in the open due to absence of proper storage infrastructure get spoiled thereby severely affecting the food security of the country. Community grain storage Banks can be a useful option under such a scenario. At least at a village or the Panchayat level these should be established to provide the peoples of that very Panchayat food grains at subsidized rates. The whole process of management and functioning of such banks should rest with the grass root level organizations like the Gram Gabha. In 1995, the Department of Rural Development, Government of Madhya Pradesh came up with such a scheme of establishing a community grain bank in the largely tribal Jhabua district of Madhya Pradesh. Such was the performance of the scheme that two years later it was adopted in all the villages under the Integrated Watershed Development Programme. Such programmes can be linked with MGNREGA; which besides ensuring food security of the locals can also help in the creation of productive assets abd providing employment to locally available men power. This is also necessary in order to ensure repayment of borrowed grain by the beneficiaries of any.

5.1.3 Food Coupons

For Public Distribution System to work effectively it is necessary to store food grains in a safe mode, which we do not due to lack of infrastructure. Also such a gigantic system of food procurement and distribution is a difficult task for any government. An other alternative to this system is the Food coupons. It is a means whereby we can ensure that subsidized food grains can be made available to the needy without the support of such a huge food procurement and storage system. Under this system instead of actually distributing food grains to the beneficiaries, they are distributed food coupons. Those who receive food coupons can use these coupons to buy food grains from the designated stores at subsidized rates as prescribed by the government from time to time. The government agents that sell food grains can get the food coupons cash in lieu of the subsidy they provided to the beneficiaries. The government, however have to maintain a buffer stock of food grains, so as to release food grains in the open market when food prices are high and have to purchase food grains when prices are low. In India states like Gujarat and Andhra Pradesh are already issuing Food coupons. These Coupons are issued to the beneficiaries at the time of issuance or renewal of ration cards. What is unique is that the next month's allocation is based on the coupons submitted to the fair price shop dealer. The cardholder, whose photo is affixed on the card has to be physically present when obtaining the coupons thereby greatly reducing the chances of proxy beneficiaries. Coupons are issued once a year and coupon holders are entitled to draw rice and kerosene on a monthly basis.

5.1.4 Universalizing the PDS

Universalizing the PDS and enlarge the food basket by including nutritious cereals like Jowar, bajra, ragi, maize and millets. However it has the inherent risk of diluting the focus on poor families. The procurement of huge quantities of wheat and rice to meet the requirements of universal distribution system would result in very less availability of food grains in the market leading to rise in open market prices.

5.1.5 Restructuring the FCI

In India the Food Corporation of India is the main authority vested with the delivery of food grains through a network of fair price shops. It has been seen that the benefits of the PDS are concentrated in a few states which have the required necessary infrastructure. States like Kerala having 3 per cent of the population receive 12 per cent of the total allocation of the PDS because of necessary infrastructure. Now, the various food deficient areas have become food surplus. As such the men power needs to be deployed in these areas or shifted from Punjab and Haryana to eastern parts. Decentralization procurement should be encouraged aggressively with emphasis on non-traditional areas and commodities. The new government at the center has plans to restructure the FCI by establishing different bodies for procurement, for distribution and for storage. All the schemes serving the same purpose of food grains distribution should be encouraged. The profit percentage of the honest dealers should be enhanced which can motivate others also to keep their business clean. The citizen charter should be strictly enforced for use by the citizens.

5.1.6 e-PDS

The first of its kind initiative started by Delhi government headed by Ms. Sheila Dixit started e-PDS. It was launched as an online system under which beneficiaries get details about ration details through SMS. The government also monitors movement of trucks carrying PDS food grains through Global Positioning System fitted in them to check diversion of food grains. A central control room to operate the electronic Public Distribution Supply Chain Management (e-PDSCM) system has already been established. Through this the information regarding movement of every truck from Food Corporation of India godown carrying food grains for about 17 lakh beneficiaries gets conveyed to them as well as to all concerned officials through SMS. For this the beneficiary desiring to avail the information may register his mobile number at the website of the system. The state of Punjab has also come up with this scheme to use GPS for tracing the movement of vehicles carrying PDS ration from the storage points to the PDS wholesale points.

5.1.7 The 3L Model

The local production-local procurement and local distribution model of the government of Chattisgarh has been largely acclaimed for its efficiency in terms of timely delivery and plugging diversions and leekages. Under local procurement, the government procures paddy directly from farmers. It buys through cooperative societies and procurement centers set up at the village level. It ensures that food is not wasted in procurement and storage. For four years now, Chhattisgarh has been giving 35 kg of grain comprising rice and wheat per month at a heavily subsidized rate to 3.6 million of its 4.4 million households. The ultra-poor pay Rs 1 per kg, while the poor pay 2 per kg, against the market price of 12-17 per kg. The ration card is the document that enables this subsidized transfer.

The whole process is guided through by use of ICT. It controls diversion and leakage in the delivery mechanism. In 2007-08, Government of Chhattisgarh computerized whole food grain supply chain from procurement of paddy at 1532 purchase centers to transportation of PDS commodities to 10416 Fair Price Shops for further distribution 3.7 million ration card holders. As an outcome of the project, 0.78 Million farmers have received computer generated cheques without any delay. Citizen participation has been increased in monitoring PDS. The use of Global Positioning System (GPS) to trace the movement of trucks also ensures that the food grains are not lost midway. The state of Chattisgarh has managed all this very efficiently. It provides food security to its population and enacted the food security act much before the central food security act came in force. It covers ninety per cent of the population unlike the central act which covers only sixty seven percent of the population. It implemented the act at a cost of 1.4 per cent of the Gross State Domestic Product (GSDP). What is credible is that the state of Chattisgarh ranks in the top three best performing states in critical fiscal parameters and management including maintaining fiscal discipline and sustainable debt management. Due to all these measures the annual growth rate of the state during eleventh plan was 8.4 per cent.

5.1.8 National Food Security Act

The National Food Security Law was passed by the parliament and it aims to provide sixty seven percent of the total Indian population the legal right to food security. It has been discussed in this book in another chapter. However, for achieving food security, we have also to increase our domestic food grain production. It would require an increase in agricultural output by 20-25 million tonnes for which it would require an investment of rupees 1,10,600 crore in various areas. More emphasis has to be laid on creating infrastructure for food grains storage and rain fed areas which constitute more than half of the total cultivable land and have a significant share in the total production.

Chapter 6
REVITALIZING EXTENSION SERVICES

The transfer of technology in the country has largely been through Public extension systems. At the central level there is the Ministry of Agriculture and Cooperatives that runs various programmes and at the state level; the states have their own extension machinery which runs through extension professionals. As agriculture is a state subject, the states therefore, have their own Department of Agriculture that runs with the respective Directorates of Agriculture and allied departments. The Indian Council of Agricultural Research (ICAR) is the apex institute that is also engaged in transfer of technology through various agricultural universities, various research and extension institutes. The state agriculture universities also work in close collaboration with respective state government in ensuring that the technology reaches the farmers well in time. The public extension system contributed a lost in bringing Green revolution in the country. But, now owing to the vast majority of farmers remaining outside the domain of extension services, the relevance of the public extension system has been questioned.

The 59th round of the National Sample Survey (NSSO, 2005) provided valuable insights into reach of extension services across India. The data collected from 51,770 households in 6638 villages showed that sixty per cent of farmer households did not access any information on modern technology that year. For the farmers who accessed information, progressive farmers and the input dealers were the main source of information. Broadcast media was also used a great deal to obtain information, which included radio, television and newspapers. The public sector extension worker was a source of information for only 5.7 per cent of farmer households interviewed. This was followed by the Krishi Vigyan Kendra (KVK) which was an extension source for only 0.7 per cent of the sample farmers. Only 0.6 per cent of the farmers accessed the extension services through Private agencies and NGO's. Access to information is identified as one of the key enablers of enhancing agricultural productivity growth. The NSSO, 2003 survey also revealed that only 40 per cent of farmer households have access to one or more sources of information. Of the sixteen different sources for accessing information on modern technology for farming, about 16.7 per cent of the farmers got their information on a daily basis from other progressive farmers in their villages. Farmers also consider input dealers (13.1 per cent), radio (13.0 per cent) and television (9.3 per cent) as important sources of information. This survey was conducted from January to December 2003; mobiles were then not used as a source of information. The survey covered 51,770 households spread over 6,638 villages across the country. A large interstate disparity existed in respect of access to information from extension workers; for instance only 0.4 per cent of the farmers in Bihar were approaching the extension workers for information, while for farmers in the state of Chhattisgarh it was 15.5 per cent. The ratio of staff to farmers also varies widely across the country (1:300 in Kerala, 1:2,000 in Rajasthan) (Raabe, 2008). The 2003 survey also pointed out that access to information from any source increased with larger farm size. Most farmers sought information on seeds. In terms of differences in source of information for the forty per cent of farmers who had accessed information smallholders famers relied primarily on other progressive farmers, input dealers and radio for information, while medium and large sized farmers equally used radio, TV and newspapers. It also revealed that contact with extension workers for medium sized and large sized farmers was almost double than that of small holder farmers (Adhiguru, Birthal and Ganesh Kumar, 2009). It is still not understood that why marginal and small farmers do not access information more frequently. Is the information unavailable, not relevant or they do not have the means to use this information.

Table 17: Percentage of Farm Households Accessing Information on Modern Agricultural Technologies from different Sources

Sl.No.	Source of Information	Percentage of Households
1	Progressive farmers	16.7
2	Input dealers	13.1
3	Radio	13.0
4	Television	9.3
5	Newspaper	7.0
6	Public Extension worker	5.7
7	Primary Cooperative society	3.0
8	Output buyers/food processors	2.3
10	Krishi Vigyan Kendra	0.7
11	NGOs and Private Agencies	0.6

Source: NSSO 2005.

6.1 Conventional vs. Agriculture Innovation Systems Approach

Agricultural development depends on innovation. The innovations are a prerequisite for agricultural development which ultimately is the route for rural development. From what once was perceived as new practice; innovations are now defined as what comes out of the interaction between different stakeholders. The goal of the research personnel's is now to facilitate the interaction between different stakeholders. The traditional approach to fostering innovation in agriculture has been until few years back one way or linear. Seldom was the knowledge of the community for whom the innovations were meant taken into consideration. Let me take an example. An innovation comes in the form of a new disease resistant and high yielding variety of a particular crop. The extension services were than supposed to make aware and advise farmers through demonstrations and other methods that a more disease-resistant variety is available, and farmers plant it. This approach encouraged the research and extension to act independently. Such was the extent of independence that two groups appeared relatively isolated with the farmer did not even seen anywhere in the picture. The one way approach also had the possibility of excluding the stakeholders like agricultural universities, informal networking among farm communities, private sector participation, agribusiness, traders, and nongovernmental and civil society organizations. It often ignores actors such as the private sector and does not always take institutions or local Indigenous technical Knowledge (ITK). The result was that the adoption of the innovation was either very slow or very less. Broad-based, sustained agricultural growth and poverty reduction require an interactive approach to agricultural development to bring in the relevant actors, organizations, and institutions, which all play a role in this process.

Now we talk of the agriculture innovations system approach. The agricultural innovation system (AIS) approach is defined as a network of organizations, enterprises, and individuals focused on bringing new products, new processes, and new forms of organization into economic use, together with the institutions and policies that affect their behavior and performance. A few decades ago, practitioners began to use the concept of innovation systems to explain noteworthy economic performance driven by a strong orientation to innovation in some developed countries.

The World Bank (2006) defines an innovation system as 'a network of organizations, enterprises, and individuals focused on bringing new products, new processes, and new forms of organization into economic use, together with the institutions and policies that affect their behavior and performance'. This thinking recognizes that interactions of people and ideas catalyze innovation and that innovation consists of generating, accessing, and putting knowledge into use (Hall 2006). It also recognizes the importance of institutions and policy in fostering innovation.

6.2 Innovations in Agricultural Extension

6.2.1 Broad Based Extension

Extension system which in the yesteryears was limited only to specific commodities like field crops has now broadened its ambit to include horticultural crops, animal husbandry, fisheries, etc. Narrow focus of extension system has now been widened and extension is no more limited to major cereals and providing subsidized inputs. Emphasis is on to introduce neglected crops such as coarse cereals and minor horticulture crops into the farming system. New technologies focusing on environment and sustainability like IPM, organic farming, natural resource management etc, were adequately promoted by the project. Moreover, new extension system could divert its attention from distribution of subsidized inputs to transferring the complete technology to farmers.

6.2.2 ICT-Enabled Tools

Agriculture is one of the core sectors where ICT interventions can be exploited a lot. Information and communication technology enabled tools have become more relevant in agricultural innovation systems. These appear ideally suited to the task of enhanced interaction because they can expand communication, cooperation, and ultimately innovation among the growing array of actors in agriculture. They are now all pervasive have reached at the gross root levels. Expanded telecommunications networks have increased the speed, reliability, and accuracy of information exchange through text, voice, and applications between farmers and other stakeholders. Now various private sector enterprises have started using ICT for the benefit of farming communities. The e-Choupal of Indian Tobacco Company (ITC), Warna village wired project of MS Swaminathan Foundation limited Chennai, Tata Kissan Sanchar Limited, Reuters Market Lights (RML) are some of the private sector initiatives in the country,

6.2.3 Expert Systems

Farmers in India often do not get the relevant technology in time. They are not aware of the scientific production of different crops. They are also not able to select the best piece of information available to them from different sources. Making on-farm and land management decisions is often challenging for them. Expert systems are the decision support tool that guide decisions on various management practices. For example what crops to rotate, when to sow and when to harvest. It is a computer program which can be used as virtual expert to guide the growers. Expert system is a technological way to deliver theoretical knowledge for results practically. As a result, application of expert system in agriculture sector has become popular and many nations took initiative to develop different expert system.

6.2.4 Agricultural Technology Management Agency

Extension system in the country is often criticized for being more centralized and supply driven. To overcome these constraints Agricultural Technology Management Agency (ATMA) was started under the Innovations in Technology Dissemination (ITD) component of National

Table 18: Various Public Private Partnerships (PPP)

Sl.No.	PPP	Activities
1	Nuziveedu Seeds and Government of Uttar Pradesh	a. Extension services in 25 districts of Uttar Pradesh regarding Paddy and Maize crops
		b. High density cotton planting in Vidharba region of Maharashtra on 10,000 acres with 2000 farmers
2	Monsanto India Limited with state governments	a. Reached to about 9 lakh peoples throughout the country and helped to improve yields and rural incomes
3	Agriculture Finance Company Ltd. with respective state governments	a. Customized Farmers' Training and Extension, Orientation and Training programme for watershed level participants under drought prone area programme (DPAP) and integrated wastelands development programme (IWDP) in Uttar Pradesh
		b. Adoption and certification of organic agriculture management system with online traceability system of facilitation of export and domestic retail chain in Gujarat, Chhattisgarh and Haryana
4	Bayer Crop Sciences and Bharti Wal mart	a. Selection and demonstration of the most suitable varieties and agronomical practices for vegetable growing in North India; the first such project launched in Malerkotla (Punjab).
5	Syngenta and CIMMYT	a. To develop drought tolerant maize for small holders farmers in Asia
6	Dhanuka Agri tech with various state governments	a. To provide quality seeds, soil testing facilities and plant protection measures

Table 19: Some ICT based initiatives in India

Sl.No.	*Initiative*	*Activities*
1.	Gyan Dhoot	Providing more than 24 public services on a user charge basis mainly in tribal areas of Madhya Pradesh with rural cyber cafes called soochanalayas
2.	e-choupal	Providing all time relevant information to farmers on different inputs, services, markets and weather through e-choupal centers located across the country
3.	Warna Wired Village	To serve the information needs of famers on cultivation of different crops including dairy and sugarcane processing
4.	Self Employed Women Association	Women empowerment by developing and strengthening Self Help Groups
5.	Dhrishti Tele Centers	Providing information related to land records, crops and market prices
8.	Tata Kissan Sansars	One stop solution providing farmers with information about crops, markets, weather through farm resource centers
9.	Digital video	Train rural communities by short instructional videos tailored to meet local agricultural needs of rural communities
10.	Reuter's market lights	Providing information to farmers via SMS on crop prices, how to improve yields, and weather forecast
11.	Kissan Call Centers	To provide extension services to the farming community through a toll free number 1800-180-1551
12.	E-Sagu	Delivery of expert advice to farmers by getting the crop status in the form of digital photographs
13.	IKSL	An initiative of IFFCO to provide timely information to farmers through mobiles including value added services also

Table 20: Various Expert Systems being put in use in Agriculture and related sectors

Sl.No.	*Expert System*	*Purpose*
1.	POMME	To advise growers about when and what to spray on their apples to avoid infestations and provides advice regarding treatment of winter injuries, drought control and multiple insect problems.
2.	UNU-AES	To support land-use officials, research scientists, farmers, and other individuals interested in maximizing benefits gained from applying agro-forestry management techniques in developing countries.
3.	CUPTEX	For cucumber production
4.	NEPER WHEAT	An expert system for irrigated wheat management
5.	TOMATEX	An expert system for tomatoes
6.	LIMEX	A Multimedia Expert System for Lime Production
7.	CITEX	An expert system for orange production
8.	MAIZE/NAPRA	Developed by Penn State University to help extension agents and agribusiness personnel identify pest management strategies in field corn for their clientele. NAPRA (National Pesticide Risk Assessment)
9.	SOYBUG,	To advise farmers on control of four important insect pests of soybeans: velvet bean caterpillar, stink bug, corn earworm, and soybean looper.
10.	SOYPEST	To provide IPM decision support to the farmers through the internet. This has been used for the crops grown in different regions of India. It provides diagnosis of pest and its preventive and curative measures
11.	3PG	Help forest managers predict tree growth for a range of species. The model calculates total above and below-ground carbon fixed in a tree stand. It uses standard weather data and information about soil depth and water-holding characteristics to calculate the energy absorbed by forest canopies converted it into biomass production.
12.	APSIM	APSIM (The Agricultural Production Systems Simulator) is a farming systems model that simulates the effects of environmental variables and management decisions on crop yield, profits and the environment.
13.	GrassGro	Using information about soils, climate, animals and pasture species, it predicts the quantity and quality of feed and animal production for a specific paddock. It assesses the production risk of different combinations of pasture and animals for different soil and climatic conditions.
14.	CABLA (Carbon Balance)	A forest growth model that links carbon, water and nitrogen flows through the atmosphere, trees and soil to estimate tree growth and carbon storage in plantations and managed forests.

Agricultural Technology Project (NATP). It functions as a registered society at District level, serving as a focal point for integrating research and extension activities at the district level and helps in decentralizing the management of agricultural technology transfer. The project involved adopting bottom up planning procedures for setting the research and extension agency in order to make the technology dissemination farmer driven and farmer accountable. ATMA aims at bottom up planning, creating farmer advisory committee to improve feedback, encouraging NGO's and private sector involvement in technology transfer, validation and refinement of technologies through research units in the district, in-service training to increase staff competence and formation and strengthening of farmer's interest group.

6.2.5 Partnerships

In the country main responsibility for agricultural extension is with respective state governments. But the present times witnessed a decline in the extension services. There were many reasons for this. The situation demanded alternative extension approaches which are demand driven, client oriented and farmer led. The than union minister Sh. Ajit Singh had also remarked that, it is now believed that the task of managing agriculture in the future cannot be adequately addressed by the public extension agencies alone, but will require the combined strengths and synergies of a pluralistic, multi-agency system in which the private corporate sector, farmers organizations, co-operatives, NGO's, para professionals, small agri business, self-help groups, input dealers and suppliers, electronic and print media and information technology will each contribute according to its own strength and capabilities.

In certain countries extension services were totally privatized. In many other countries different forms of privatization like the cost sharing, voucher, franchisee and other arrangements were put in place. In a country where more than eighty per cent of the farmers were small and marginal complete privatization is not a feasible. As such today greater stress is laid on partnerships. Partnerships provide synergistic approach in the extension approach. In first of its kind a public private partnership (PPP) known as the Hoshangabad model came into limelight in India in 2001. In this model private sector pioneer in plant protection chemicals Dhanuka ltd. entered into MoU with the Director of Agriculture, state of Madhya Pradesh for providing technical knowhow to the farming community. Both are working together in areas like soil testing, training, farmers' tour programmes, demonstrations, transfer of technology through cyber dhabas, establishment of markets and facilitating in providing credit facilities to farmers.

The central government has also issued a framework on Public Private Partnership for Integrated Agricultural Development (PPPIAD) under the Rashtriya Krishi Vikas Yojana to state governments. The states now have the flexibility to team up with private sector players on large scale integrated projects related to agriculture that provide end to end solutions from production to marketing. The Small Farmers' Agribusiness Consortium (SFAC), an off shoot of the Agriculture Ministry has been nominated as a National Level Agency to examine the proposals from technical viewpoint and thereafter propose it for funding to the concerned state. However, the final decision on the type and number of projects to be supported under PPPIAD has been left entirely to the states. The projects can last for three to five years and corporate firms are also required to mobilize farmers into producer groups, build agricultural infrastructure, value addition, marketing and technology solutions to farmers.

6.2.6 Market Led Extension

The increased competitiveness of the Indian agriculture and in order to maintain the edge of the farmers in the market it is necessary that farmers have to transform themselves from mere producers cum sellers in the domestic market to organized market driven production. This is also necessary to meet the consumer demand and to realize the better returns on investments, risks and efforts. For this the extension personnel's' are now facilitating appropriate linkages of the farmer or commodity interest groups with the markets so that they can earn handsomely. Market-led-extension system establishes its position by helping the farmers realize high returns for the produce and minimize the production cost and improve the product value as marketability.

6.2.7 Volunteer Farmer Trainers Extension

This approach has also been found effective in providing timely information to the farming community. Studies done at the World Agro forestry Center and the International Livestock Research Institute had revealed that the voluntary farmer trainers are effective agents of change. Voluntary farmer trainers are trained by research and extension institutes. These are highly effective training on an average 20 farmers per month. As these have an in depth knowledge of the prevailing local culture and practices, speak their language and thus instill a greater confidence in them. This helps in adoption of technology rapidly. Here the farmer himself is the agent of change and the extension workers serving as the facilitators of change.

In an agrarian country like India, innovation is necessary for increasing productivity of major crops so that the competitiveness of Indian agriculture can be maintained and desired economic growth can be achieved. This will than further help in alleviating poverty, generating income, ensuring food security and social equity for all. To conclude if we are to cope up with the challenges in the agriculture sector both at the national as well as global level we must have to innovate continuously and this approach can be used effectively.

6.2.8 Farmer Field Schools

The farmer field schools are yet another innovation in agricultural extension where farmers themselves learn from the field conditions by observing the daily events in their fields. Learning takes place in groups and there are master trainers. After watching keenly the crop conditions at different stages they themselves arrive at conclusions. The farmers in groups of 5 to 6 go in the fields and analyze their crop conditions. After the careful observation of field conditions each farmer groups analyses its own way and then presents it in the group. Based on this report discussions take place with the master trainers acting as a facilitators. After the discussion has taken place a final course of action is drawn and then acted upon. Farmer Field Schools (FFS) are a unique example of Farmer led extension. As learning is a group activity and field based which empowers farmers to solve their field problems by themselves. It helps in fostering a spirit of empowerment in them.

6.3 Revitalizing Extension Services

6.3.1 Privatization

The low level of outreach of public extension services is partly due to the public staff being overburdened with implementing state and centralized schemes, (Sulaiman Hall, and Suresh 2005). The problem gets further compounded by insufficient funds for operational costs, training, and capacity development, which limits the activities and continual development of the extension staff. Of the required 1.3 million to 1.5 million extension personnel required, there are only about 100,000 on the job (Working Group on Agricultural Extension 2007).

Privatization of extension services has been now practiced in many countries. Privatization at different places is in the form of Franchisee, Vouchers, Contracting, Cost sharing, Cost recovery, Outsourcing etc. Contracting is considered to be one of the most feasible options for privatizing the economies of developing countries. Government can assign contract to nonprofit voluntary organizations for various types of services. It has emerged as one such promising institutional framework for the delivery of price incentives, technology and other agricultural inputs. Similarly Hindustan Lever issued contracts to farmers in northern India to grow selected varieties of tomatoes. But private sector has its own compulsions. It usually operates when the situation is conducive for it. It will not favour working in resource poor areas where farmers are reluctant to pay for the extension services. In India too where sixty per cent of the area is rainfed and more than eighty per cent of the farmers are marginal and small privatization cannot be the best alternative. One option suggested by Swanson (2008) was that the private sector could serve the needs of medium size and commercial farmers, while the public sector could work in remote areas, which are currently not serviced well.

6.3.2 Overcoming the Shortage of Extension Functionaries

Presently there is a huge dearth of extension functionaries at the gross root level to carry out the extension work as a result of which the extension work gets affected severely. To overcome this shortage, Para technicians can be very helpful. Para technicians are persons without professional degrees but trained in specific skills) do provide services for a fee in a particular area such as artificial insemination, grafting, etc and charge for the service. To overcome the shortage of extension functionaries the concept of Para extension workers is a useful option. India has now more than six lakh villages and about 2.5 lakh Panchayats. About 80 per cent of the members of the Panchayat are farmers. A certain number of volunteers can be picked from each Panchayat and trained by the nearest

KVK or the state department of agriculture regarding the new technology in agriculture and allied fields. Their field of work can be expanded to include other rural development programmes also.

Similarly the Input dealers are also important agents of the transfer of technology. They play a pivotal role in not only supplying the inputs but also in getting farmers to adopt the new technology. India has around 3 lakh agri-input dealers, out of which around 85 to 90 per cent do not have any formal education. For these three lakh input dealers having immense importance in disseminating agricultural technology National Institute of Agricultural Extension Management Hyderabad has started a One year Diploma programme in Agricultural extension services for input dealers. It can go a long way in increasing the outreach of extension services. Instead of reaching out to 12 crore farmers we can easily reach the input dealers.

6.3.3 National Mission on Agricultural Extension and Technology (NMAET)

The government of India has launched the National Mission on Agricultural Extension and Technology (NMAET) during the 12th Plan period. The NMAET consists of four Sub Missions. These are Sub-Mission on Agricultural Extension (SMAE), Sub-Mission on Seed and Planting Material (SMSP), Sub Mission on Agricultural Mechanization (SMAM) and finally Sub Mission on Plant Protection and Plant Quarantine (SMPP). The ATMA was launched with the objective of strengthening extension machinery and utilizing it for synergizing research and extension interventions at a single focal point. During the eleventh five year plan the dissemination of agricultural technology was done through 17 different schemes of Department of Agriculture and Cooperation. The NMAET has been envisaged as the next step towards the dissemination of agricultural technology. The recommendation of the Working Group of the Planning Commission and suggestions and inputs received from wide consultations with different stakeholders formed the basis of mission document of NMAET. For all the sub missions we need technology and its dissemination As such they are linked to each other at the field level and most components thereof have to be disseminated among farmers and other stakeholders through a strong extension network. The aim of the Mission is to restructure and strengthen agricultural extension to enable delivery of appropriate technology and improved agronomic practices to farmers. For this besides the expending the physical outreach use of ICT, formation of Farmers Interest Groups (FIGs), Farmers Producer Organizations (FPOs) and partnerships are encouraged. Public-Private-Partnership is encouraged in the Extension and Training components of the Mission. For this credible Non-Governmental Organizations (NGOs), para-extension workers, Farmers Organizations etc. are encouraged to participate and provide extension and training services and guidance to farmers to improve agricultural production and productivity. The input dealers' and-agripreneurs are also trained to give advisories to the farmers.

Chapter 7
AGRICULTURE AND POVERTY REDUCTION

Dr. Sarvepalli Radhakrishnan, the first vice president of Republic of India had once remarked that a free India would be judged by the way it served the interests of the common people in terms of food, clothing, shelter and social services. Unfortunately after more than sixty years of his remarks we still are not able to provide food to our population. While it is beyond any dispute that poverty has declined over the years, the percentage decline in poverty is disputable. The percentage decline in poverty has been well below anticipated.

7.1 Poverty Trend and Food Grain Availability

Official statistics show that poverty measured in terms of Head count ratio declined from 54.9 per cent in 1973-74 to only 27.5 per cent in 2004-05 as is evident from Table 21. Further, this estimate increased to 37.2 per cent when the Tendulkar committee applied a poverty line of rupees 446.68 per capita per month for rural areas instead of rupees 356.30 per capita per month and rupees 578.80 per capita per month for urban areas at 2004-05 prices. In other words a small increase in poverty line of rupees 90 and rupees 40 per capita per month in rural and urban areas respectively led to massive increase in the estimated population in poverty of almost 10 percentage points. The estimates for 2009-10 are that as much as 29.8 per cent of the country's population is in poverty based on Tendulkar methodology. The per capita net food grain availability was 480.3 gm during 1987-91 and experienced a reduction every five year and reached 440.4 gm during 2007-2010 (Table 22). Even if we distribute the food grains equally among the population each person will still not meet the requirement of 480 grams as recommended by Indian Council of Medical Research (2010) for persons engaged in moderate activity. The calories and protein intake of the rural poorest 30 per cent households have also declined in the last decade.

Table 21: Poverty Trend in India from 1973-74 to 2004-05

Year	*Percentage of Population Below Poverty Line*	*Total Poverty (in millions)*
1973-74	54.9	321.3
1977-78	51.3	328.9
1983	44.5	322.9
1987-88	38.9	307.1
1993-94	36.0	320.3
1999-00	26.1	260.2
2004-05	27.5	301.7
2004-05 **	37.2	407.2
2009-10**	29.8	354.68

Source: Mehta, A. K, 2013.

*Tendulkar committee report

Table 22: Trend in per Person Net Cereal Availability (in gm)

Years (Average)	*Per Person Net Cereal Availability (in gm)*	*Per Person Net Pulse Availability (in gm)*	*Per Person Net Food Grain Availability (in gm)*
1987-91	440.7	39.6	480.3
1992-96	439.3	35.6	474.9
1997-2001	423.7	33.6	457.3
2002-06	419.6	32.9	452.4
2007-10*	403.9	36.5	440.4

Source: Sainath, 2012.

Table 23: Calories and Protein Intake of the Rural Poorest Thirty per cent Households

Average Calories Intake (Kcal)		*Average Protein Intake (grams)*	
1993-94	2004-05	1993-94	2004-05
1687	1655	47	46

Source: NSSO, 2005.

Jean Dreze, a member of the National Advisory Council calls Hunger as a hidden national emergency. What is shocking is that 25 member states of the sub-Saharan region are better off than India in terms of food security and we are even worse off than Pakistan. About 410 million peoples are poor and food insecure in just eight Indian states and this number is more than in the 26 Sub-Saharan countries as per a report of the Oxford University (Hazra, 2012). There is not a single state with low or even moderate levels of hunger. The so called food bowl Punjab falls in serious category and ranks behind Vietnam and Saudi Arabia.

7.2 The Food Grain Scenario in India

Future Projections in India

Since 1960-61, India's total food grain production has increased at an annual growth rate of 2.68 per cent and it is mainly due to increase in yield (growth rate being 2.44 per cent as against growth rate of area being 0.17 per cent per annum during 1960-61 to 1998-99). To project the future food grains supply, past growth trend were extrapolated by Goyal and Singh (2002). They expected the food grain supply to be about 245, 291 and 342 million tonnes by 2010, 2020 and 2030 AD, respectively. To meet the projected demand in the year 2020 country must have to increase the yields per hectare as the possibility of expansion of area and livestock population are minimal.

7.3 Millennium Development Goals (MDGs)

As a renewed commitment towards human development the Millennium Development Goals were adopted by the United Nations member states in 2000. The Millennium Development Goals (MDGs) and targets come from the Millennium Declaration, signed by 189 countries, including 147 heads of State and Government, in September 2000. The declaration includes eight Millennium Development Goals (MDGs) each with quantified targets, to motivate the international community and provide an accountability mechanism for actions taken to enable millions of poor people to improve their livelihoods.

About 70 per cent of the MDGs target group lives in rural areas, particularly in Asia and Africa, and for them agriculture is a crucial component on whom their livelihood depend. Immediate gains in poor households' welfare can be achieved through agriculture, which can help the poor overcome some of the critical constraints they now face in meeting their basic needs. A report of the inter agency and expert group on MDG indicators led by UN DESA came out with the findings that poverty rates and number of people living in extreme poverty have decreased in every region of the world including sub saharan Africa. Although a considerable progress has been made in achieving the MDGs, yet the statistics does not favour India.

7.4 Reducing Poverty via Agriculture

According to a USAID document (1995), "Global agriculture currently produces ample calories and nutrients to provide all the world's population healthy and productive lives". A successful strategy for alleviating poverty and hunger in developing countries must by recognizing that these are mainly rural phenomenon and that agriculture is at heart of livelihoods of rural people. Today 75 per cent of poor people in developing countries live in rural areas. In 2020, the majority of world's population is projected to live in urban areas but 60 per cent of poverty will still be rural poverty (IFAD: Rural Poverty Report). Hunger and poverty reduction require that the incomes of poor peoples and the sources from which they derive their livelihoods be enhanced. According to Kostas Stamoulis, Director, FAO Agriculture Development Economics Division, most of the extreme poor depend on agriculture and related activities for a significant part of their livelihoods. Agriculture growth involving small holders especially women will be most effective in reducing extreme hunger and poverty when it increases returns to labour and generates employment for the poor. A world development report also said that GDP growth emanating from agriculture is more effective in reducing poverty. Our Prime Minister also said that inflation hurts the weakest sections of society the most and there can be no better anti poverty programme than developing agriculture which has the potential to arrest rising food prices and contain inflation. Therefore the pro poor income growth needs to be encouraged. But the question is under what circumstances is income growth pro poor and the answer definitely is the income growth originating from agriculture is pro poor and will reduce poverty. The experience of poverty reduction in poor agrarian societies reveals that a key requirement to overcome poverty is by raising the productivity of small scale farmers.

Table 24: Incidence of Hunger and Poverty by Farm Size in Rural India

Size of Land Holdings (in ha)	*Per cent of Population*	
	Hungry	*Poor*
Less than 0.5	49	54
0.5 to 1	32	38
1.0 to 2.0	24	27
2.0 to 4.0	17	19
More than 4	12	14

Source: IARI-FAO/RAP study 2001 based on NSSO 50th round, 1993-94, quoted in Agri policy vision 2020.

Several studies in India too revealed that raising agricultural productivity can enhance growth and employment in rural non farm sector and thereby contribute to poverty reduction. An analysis of the incidence of rural poverty and hunger by farm size revealed that more than half of the landless people are poor. Poverty got significantly reduced from 54 per cent in the landless group to 38 per cent in the sub-marginal group, suggesting that even a small piece of land, less than 1/2 hectare, can greatly reduce both poverty and hunger (Table 24). The incidence of hunger and poverty gets reduced as one is able to meet even part of his/her dietary energy requirement through growing his/her own food. Studies show that even a small plot of one's own helps women to escape extreme poverty and deprivation.

There has been a significant reduction in poverty ratio in states like Andhra Pradesh, Kerala, Madhya Pradesh, Odisha etc. States like Punjab and Haryana have also been successful in reducing their poverty by following modernization path and high agricultural growth rate (Sarma, A., 2013). The experience from BRICS countries indicates that a one percentage growth in agriculture is at least two to three times more effective in reducing poverty than the same growth emanating from non-agriculture sectors. Since agriculture forms the resource base for a number of agro-based industries and agro-services, it would be more meaningful to view agriculture not as farming alone but as a holistic value chain, it needs a focused approach from soil management, cultivation of crops to providing post harvest infrastructure processing, and value addition and marketing. All this will create more employment opportunities for the rural masses besides improving the profitability of the agricultural sector ultimately reducing the poverty and malnutrition. While agriculture is vital for and has a direct bearing for achieving the first MDG, *i.e.*, eradicating extreme hunger and poverty it is also related directly or indirectly with other MDGs also Thus, a necessary component in meeting the MDGs by 2015 in many parts of the world is a more productive and profitable agricultural sector. Given that India is still home to the largest number of poor and malnourished people in the world, a higher priority to agriculture will achieve the goals of reducing poverty and malnutrition as well as of inclusive growth.

7.5 Right to Food and Food Security Act

Government of India gave the Right to Food to peoples in the country by enacting 'Food security act' that entitles food to about two third of the population at an affordable cost so as to ensure that all Indians "live a life with dignity". The act marks a shift in approach to the problem of food security; from the current 'welfare paradigm' to a 'rights-based approach'. The legislation confers eligible beneficiaries the legal right to receive grain at highly subsidized prices. The act provides for five kilogram per person per family subject to a maximum of 25 kg per family. The act brings under its purview 75 per cent of rural households and 50 per cent of urban households. The beneficiaries would receive five kilograms of subsidized food grains at the rate of rupees three per kilogram for rice, Wheat for rupees two per kilogram and coarse cereals for rupees one per kilogram.

7.6 Food Security Act: Some Concerns

No doubt, we have done a remarkable thing by making food security act. But serious concerns have been raised about the sustainability of this act. Is it sustainable to continue with huge amounts of subsidies? Can't those subsidies be used for investing in agricultural research and providing the necessary infrastructure? For the implementation of this act we need to identify the bottom 67 per cent of the population. Will this exercise be an authentic one without any inclusion as well as exclusion error? It would have been better if the act would have been made universal excluding only top income groups (tax payers) which would have been easily identified. Farmers can also go for cultivating crops which are more profitable than paddy, wheat and maize and in turn get these crops at subsidized rates under PDS. Production can also be affected if the farmers stop producing food grains for self consumption if they will get these at throw away prices. In extreme cases if the government has to import the food grains to meet the food security act obligations then will it not lead to price rise. The WTO has also laid down that the subsidies cannot be more than 10 per cent of the total food grains production. How will we ensure that we do not go beyond that limit. All these and many more questions which definitely the policy makers have to keep in mind before finally delivering the things.

7.7 Food Security and Population

Today when we talk of food security, we think of increasing our productivity by all possible means. But one thing we do not consider is the burgeoning population. Unless and until we check the population growth we cannot make every person food secure. Infact policy makers have disregarded this fact that the food problem can also be addressed by controlling population growth. A balance between increasing food production and controlling population could also be a viable strategy (Kang, 2013). Indian population in 2012 was 120.51 crore (17.3 per cent of world population) and China population in the same year was 134.32 crore (20 per cent of the world's population). But the figures taken out from the report of US Census Bureau revealed that in 2025 India with population of 139.60 crore will surpass China's population of 139.46 crore. What is disheartening is that Indian population will continue to grow whereas China's population would start declining after 2030. The population predicted for India and China in 2050 are 165.66 crore and 130.37 crore respectively. This is definitely an alarming situation and policy makers and planners need to formulate policies and programmes so as to minimize the population.

This increasing population has one positive aspect too and that is the demographic dividend. This was acknowledged by US president Barrack Obama too when on his visit to India in 2010 had said the India is fortunate to have more than 50 per cent of young population. The need is to tap this demographic dividend by ensuring that they have proper access to education, health, food and their basic necessities. The youth can be moulded to take on farming as an enterprise and become job providers rather than job seekers.

Chapter 8
FIGHTING CLIMATE CHANGE

Scientific studies have revealed beyond any doubt that the climate is changing and becoming more unpredictable. Climate Change having pervasive and complex negative effect on water resources, air and water quality, fisheries and agriculture and food production is the most serious environmental threat looming large over the planet today (Dar, D.W. 2009). It is now being recognized as unequivocal, more so in terms of increasing temperature and carbon dioxide concentration, melting of glaciers and rising of average global sea levels. The fourth assessment report of the Inter governmental Panel on Climate Change stated that eleven of the last 12 years (1995 to 2006) were among the warmest years in the records of global surface temperature since 1850. The increase in the concentration of greenhouse gases (GHGs) (Table 27) in the atmosphere has resulted in warming of the global climate by 0.74°C between 1906 and 2005. The mean temperature in India is projected to increase up to 1.7°C in kharif (July to October) and up to 3.2°C during rabi (November to March) season, while the mean rainfall is expected to increase by 10 per cent by 2070 (Pathak *et al.*, 2012). Global mean sea level rise at 1.8 mm per year and since 1993 at 3.1 mm per year with contributions from thermal expansion, melting glaciers and the ice caps. The annual average Arctic sea ice extent has shrunk by 2.7 per cent per decade with larger decreases in summer of 7.4 per cent per decade. Agriculture contributes to climate change as well as is affected by it. Agriculture is extremely vulnerable to climate change. Rise in temperature reduces the crops yields without minimizing weeds, diseases or other challenges. Change in rainfall pattern also increases the likelihood of short term crop failures. Although there will be gains in some crops in some regions of the world but the overall impact of climate change on agriculture is expected to be negative threatening the global food security (Nelson et al. 2009). Stern (2005) using formal economic models estimated that in the absence of effective counteractive measures, the costs and risk of climate change will be equivalent to 5 per cent decrease in Global Gross Domestic Product. On a wider range the damage could rise to 20 per cent decrease in GDP which can increase the risk of famine in poorest countries. Atkinson et al. (2008) also predicted that climate change would have adverse impacts on food production, food quality and food security. By 2080, the number of undernourished people in different parts of the globe is shown below in the Table 25. Another complication arising out of the rising temperature is climate refugees. Climate refugees constitute a segment of 'environmental refugee'. Myers and Kent described environmental refugees as persons who no longer gain a secure livelihood in their traditional homelands because of what are primarily environmental factors of unusual scope. These refugees no longer gain a secure livelihood because of several factors that include drought, soil erosion, deforestation etc. Climate refugees on the other hand are forced to leave their homes because of the effects of climate change and global warming. It is estimated that the number of those affected by extremities of weather would be as much as 200 million. A study by Dr. Hefin Jones of Cardiff University

Table 25: Expected Number of Undernourished Population (in millions) Incorporating the Effects of Climate

Sl.No.	*Region*	*Population (in millions)*			
		1990	*2020*	*2050*	*2080*
1.	Developing countries	885	772	579	554
2.	Asia Developing	659	390	123	73
3.	Sub-Saharan Africa	138	273	359	410
4.	Latin America	54	53	40	23
5.	Middle east and North Africa	33	55	56	48

Source: Tubiello and Fischer, 2007.

revealed that in India there would be about 30 million peoples that would be the victim of environmental atrocities. In the coming times about 15 million peoples in Bangladesh and about 30 million peoples in china would have to leave their homes due to rising sea levels and soil erosion (Panigrahi, 2014). The magnitude of such climate induced change being very vast could severely affect food security of the burgeoning population.

Global Warming

It simply refers to the increase in temperature of earth due to excessive increase in the concentration of Green house gases (GHGs). These Green House Gases do not allow the solar radiations to go back into the atmosphere. The radiative energy leaving the planetary surface (earth) is absorbed by these Green House Gases thus creating a Green House Effect. Besides earth, the atmosphere of Venus and Mars also contain GHGs. The GHG's how ever covering the earth like a blanket (Table 26) and if there were no GHGs, the earth would have been 31° Celsius cooler than it is now.

Table 26: Major Green House Gases (GHG's) and their Principal Sources

Carbon dioxide	Fossil fuel (Coal, oil, natural gas), solid wastes, tree, wood products, chemical reactions like manufacture of cement
Methane	Production of coal, oil, natural gas, livestock, decay of organic waste, municipal wastes, landfills
Nitrous oxide	Agricultural fertilizers, combustion of fossil fuel,solid wastes
Fluorinated gases (Hydrofluorocarbons, SF6, per fluorocarbons called as high Global warming potential gases	Industrial processes, Refrigerated gases,Air conditioners

8.1 How Agriculture Contributes to Climate Change

Of the different gases that are responsible for rising temperatures, it has been found that carbon dioxide contributes sixty percent, methane fifteen per cent and Nitrous oxide five percent to global warming. There are so many agricultural practices that lead to release of these gases. The figures in Table 27 clearly show how their concentration has been increasing in the atmosphere. Agriculture practices like shifting cultivation that include felling of trees and clearing large tracts for growing crops,

Table 27: Abundance and Lifetime of Greenhouse Gases in the Atmosphere

Parameters	CO_2	CH_4	NO_2	*Chlorofluoro-carbons*
Average concentration (100 years ago)	290,000	900	270	0
Current concentration (ppbV)	380,000	1774	319	5
Projected concentration in 2030 (ppbV)	400,000 to 500,000	2800 to 3000	400 to 500	3 to 6
Atmospheric life time	5 to 200	9 to 15	114	75
Global warming potential (100 years relative to CO_2)	1	25	298	4750 to 10,900

Source: IPCC, 2007.

burning of crop residues, traditional methods of rice cultivation and chemicals used for increasing yields and controlling diseases are the main factors that have brought this situation. The large amount of smoke being released from our factories, vehicles also carry with them various green house gases. The Nitrogenous fertilizers that are applied to the soil besides releasing methane, nitrous oxide etc. in the atmosphere also causes nitrate pollution of the water bodies. It is here worthwhile to mention that Nitrogen has a global warming potential of 296 times more than an equal mass of CO_2. Emissions also come out through the use of animal manures. Our traditional methods of Paddy cultivation, by keeping the paddy fields submerged for longer time also release Methane gas in the atmosphere. Methane is about 25-times more effective as a heat-trapping gas than CO_2. Animal digestive processes also emit Methane. In ruminant animals, methane is produced as a by-product of the digestion of feed in the rumen under anaerobic condition. The other sources of this gas are the wetlands, natural gas and oil extraction, burning of biomass and the landfills. Urban environments are islands of heat produced by industry, transport and by asphalt absorption of solar energy. Trees promote sequestration of carbon into soil and plant biomass but the large scale felling of trees more particularly in North east for growing crops is furthering Global warming.

8.2 Effect of Climate Change on Agriculture

Effect on Yield of Major Crops

Different crops respond to climate change effects differently. In case of C_3 crops the increase in CO_2 concentration up to a certain level will be beneficial as it will lead to increased photosynthesis. But the yields of major cereals crops, especially wheat are likely to be reduced. This will be due to decrease in grain filling duration, increased respiration. Further the increase in the frequency of extreme climatic events will adversely affect agricultural productivity. The climate change impact on the productivity of rice in Indian state of Punjab has revealed that with all other climatic variables remaining constant, for temperature increases of 1°C, 2°C and 3°C, there would be a corresponding reduced grain yield of rice by 5.4 per cent, 7.4 per cent and 25.1 per cent, respectively (Aggarwal *et al.*, 2009). The increased temperature and the sea level rise would also threaten the agricultural bio diversity. It has been estimated that the disappearance of different plant and animal species would be about 100-times faster than their rate of disappearance in the past. A detailed assessment of the 394 species of primates from South America to Indonesia has indicated that 29 per cent are in danger of disappearing due to hunting, habitat loss and climate change. In Northern parts in December the night temperature continues to be 7-8^{0}c and day temperature is hovering about 20^{0}C in the country. At this stage the night temperature should not be more than 4^0 C and the day temperature should not be more than 14-16^0 C. High temperature at this stage of winter stunt the growth of wheat plants and affects the tillering process. In Haryana wheat production has declined from 4106 Kg per ha in 2000-01 to 3937 Kg per ha in 2003-04 with maximum temperature rising by 3^{0}C during February- March in last seven years. An overall increase in 2^{0}c will lead to 7 per cent increase in rainfall that would lead to 8 per cent loss in farm level net revenue (Gahukar, 2009). Maize which is grown in rainfed area is also expected to hit hard by temperature rise.

Effect on Water

Due to increase in temperature there will be more evapotranspiration in certain areas south of 40^{0}North. This will also increase the demand for irrigation water and lowering of the ground water table across different regions of the country. The melting of glaciers may increase the water availability in rivers but in the long run the availability will decrease. The IPCC reports that once these glaciers disappear, the once perennial rivers would turn into seasonal ones. In the country also in the long run, water flow in the Ganges could drop by two-third affecting more than 400 million peoples who depend on it for drinking water. A study by the British

Climate Change specialists concluded that up to 85 per cent of the Amazon forests could be lost if GHGs emissions and deforestation are not brought under control and destroying the Amazon would mean converting a significant carbon sink into a major source (Ramadhar, 2009).The increase in run off can be made useful provided we have water harvesting structures. It has been estimated that water shortage due to climate change would result in about 20 per cent net decline in the rice yields in India. The water balance in different parts of India will be disturbed and the quality of groundwater along the coastal track will be affected more due to intrusion of sea waters.

Effect on Soil

Rise in temperature of the soil would increase the natural decomposition of soil organic matter and increase of the mineralization of Nitrogen but its availability will decrease due to high gaseous losses through processes like volatilization and denitrification. The organic matter content of soils in India would further lower. When temperatures rise, the crop residues have higher C: N ratio which reduces their rate of decomposition. The change in rainfall volume and frequency, and wind may change the severity, frequency and extent of soil erosion. It can also lead to salt-water ingression in the coastal lands due to rise in sea water land and higher evaporation making them unfeasible for agriculture.

Effect on Insect Pests

The increased carbon dioxide concentration in the atmosphere is being responded to by many plant species by increased photosynthetic rates and increased biomass. The plants also have decreased nutritional levels leading to their increased plant consumption rates (Bezemer *et al.*, 1998). This can result in an increased level of plant damage because the pests have to consume more plant tissue to acquire similar levels of nutrition especially in foliage feeders (Srinivasa Rao *et al.*, 2009). The rising temperatures also cause a change in the distribution of range of the crops, pests and their natural enemies. As an example the increased warming will make it feasible for the pink boll worm (*Pectinophora gossypiella*) to move from cotton to areas that are presently not fit for its survival. Predictions are that with a one degree rise in temperature the species would spread to 200 kilometers northwards or 140 meters upwards in altitude (Parry *et al.*, 1989).

Effect on Pulses

An increase in the concentration of CO_2 can have a positive impact on the pulses having C_3 mechanism by stimulating photosynthesis, enhancing fertilization and reducing water loss via plant respiration (Ali *et al.*, 2009). Yields in pulses may increase by 10-15 per cent up to a CO_2 level of 550 ppm but the higher atmospheric temperature due to higher levels will adversely affect the physiological processes and productivity. A study of John et al. 2008 to know the impact of increased temperature, reduced rainfall and increased carbon dioxide concentration in semiarid tropics of Zimbabwe using a simulation experiment revealed that the impact of increased temperature (3.1°Celsius rise in maximum and minimum temperature) could cause a yield reduction of 16 per cent in sorghum and maize and 31 and 3 per cent yield reductions in ground nut and pigeon pea respectively.

Effect on Livestock

The rising temperatures can alter the productivity of pasture and forage crops due to water scarcity. Increased temperature would increase the lignification of plant tissues thereby reducing their digestibility. The changes in rainfall pattern may also influence expansion of vectors during wetter years leading to large outbreaks of diseases. Similarly the rising temperature of sea and river water is likely to affect breeding, migration and harvests of fishes. Coral bleaching is likely to increase due to higher sea surface temperature. Under climatic stress there is a decrease in efficiency of nutrient utilization and dry matter intake. Time to attain puberty is prolonged due to decline in the growth rate at higher temperatures. Milk yield in cows is reduced by 10-25 per cent due to heat stress. Temperature and humidity with water logging are most favorable for both endo and ecto parasites and disease vectors.

8.3 Tackling Climate Change

8.3.1

To control the harmful effects of rising concentration of green house gases in the atmosphere we need both adaptation as well as mitigation strategies.

Mitigation Strategies

These strategies mostly aim at reducing the green house gas emissions from their potential source. The methane emission can be reduced from rice fields by providing mid season aeration by going for short term drainage. The organic matter in the soil can also be managed by promoting aerobic degradation through composting or by incorporating it in the fields during the off season. Pathak, 2010 has recommended site specific nutrient management to reduce emissions from nitrogenous compounds. Plant derived organics such as neem oil, neem cake and Karanja seeds act as nitrification inhibitors. Similarly mitigation of carbon dioxide, another important green house gas can be done from the atmosphere by carbon sequestration. Reducing tillage, mulching, incorporating residues all can help in sequester carbon dioxide from the soil. Sorghum can play an important role in mitigating the effects of global warming by regulating the emission of GHG's like N_2O, CO_2 and CH_4 (Madan, 2009). In Sorghum the brown mid rib varieties have lower lignin content and higher digestibility. Cultivating such varieties will greatly help in the reduction of the said gases.

Adaptation Strategies

Adaptation as defined by IPCC is 'adjustment in natural or human systems in response to actual or expected climatic stimuli or their effects which moderates harm or exploits beneficial opportunities'. The different adaptation strategies include the development of varieties tolerant to heat, salinity, stress and having resistance to flood and drought. Crop Diversification is another strategy which besides providing regular income to farmers can also offset the negative impact of climate change. Diversification also involves replacing plant types and livestock with new varieties intended for higher drought or heat tolerance, are being advocated as having the potential to increase productivity in the face of temperature and moisture stresses. Changing land-use practices to include trees also is a good alternative. Adjusting the cropping sequence, including changing the dates and time of sowing, planting and harvesting is another option. In arid and semi arid tropics the adaptation measures to reduce the negative effects of increased climatic variability include changing of the cropping calendar to take advantage of the wet period and to avoid extreme weather events (*e.g.*, typhoons and storms) during the growing season. The resource-conserving technologies (RCTs) like the rain water harvesting, recycling of household water, use of local resources like cow dung manure etc are also a key factor in reducing the impact of climate change. Studies done in the fields have shown that Resource Conserving Technologies now being adapted in the rice-wheat belt of the Indo-Gangetic Plains offer several advantages like saving of labour, water and early planting of wheat. The RCTs in rice-wheat system also have pronounced effects on mitigation of greenhouse gas emission and adaptation to climate change (Pathak *et al.*, 2009).

8.3.2 Research

Research in farmers' fields is not getting the same priority as is in university plots. Farmers still use the same seed years after years without caring for the declining productivity. Cirrado in Brazil was once discarded as a waste land and Norman Borlough had said that even grass cannot grow here. But peoples discovered bacteria that fix nitrogen in the soil, applied Limestone for about three years and then sowed soya bean. The result is that presently Brazil is the biggest exporter of Soya bean in the world (Malik, S., 2009). This is the kind of research we need here in India. We need cutting edge research on climate resilient technologies. Improvement of germplasm of different crops for heat-stress tolerance should be carried out. United States is now planning to set up ten centers across the country to be called as 'Climate Hubs' to help farmers and ranchers to adjust to the increasing frequency of extremities of weather. According to US Agriculture Secretary, the main goal of setting up these Climate hubs is to help the agriculture industry adjust to new conditions, invasive pests, flooding and drought. These will conduct risk analysis on production of crops, identify different ways that make farmers and ranchers vulnerable to swings in the climate and thus accordingly recommend new seeds or techniques to restrict the damage. The need of the hour is also to tailor such varieties which can withstand the stress. The CGIAR institutes are researching on how to make crops more tolerant to increased levels of heat. ICRISAT is also working on developing crops that are better adapted to heat and high soil temperatures. The short duration chick pea varieties like super ICC 96029 and early maturing KAK 2 can with stand high temperatures. Similarly pearl millet varieties that can flower at $40+^{0}$ C have been developed and Groundnut cultivar ICGV 91114 is the other resilient crops developed by ICRISAT.

8.3.3 Weather Based Advisories

The development of various techniques has now made it possible to stop the losses due to volatilization, nitrification and leaching. N_2 emission can be contained with the judicious use of Nitrogenous fertilizers. During 2009 over 50 lakh hectare area with rice crop suffered due to delayed monsoon and the seedling almost died which resulted in huge loss of 13 million tonnes of rice (Prabhu, 2012). Such type of losses would have been avoided, had the contingency planning been put in place. An effective weather monitoring and early warning system is also essential. The gap between the actual yield and the potential yield will have to be removed by replacing the drought prone varieties with drought resistant varieties. The states of Punjab and Haryana have begun delaying transplanting of rice to escape hottest part of summer. Alterations in crop management practices like the System of rice intensification (SRI), has in some ways make climate production more secure. The losses in wheat production from 4-5 million tons can be reduced to 1-2 million tons if farmers change to timely planting and better adopted varieties. For that, advance weather based advisories are necessary so that farmers can adjust accordingly.

8.3.4 Technology Dissemination

Farmers have to be trained and motivated for adopting various climate resilient technologies. Rain water harvesting is a necessary prerequisite in the rainfed regions of the country. Principles of increasing water infiltration along with decreasing runoff by providing vegetative covers, wind breaks etc and reducing soil evaporation with use of crop residues mulch need to be familiarized with the farming community. Agricultural extension professionals have to take eco friendly production technologies to the farmer fields. Research and extension strategies have to be synchronized so that rising temperatures can be controlled to some extent. M. S. Swaminathan has called for developing climate-resilient agriculture system with focus on the local conditions in each of the 128 agro-climatic zones in the country. Describing 'Agriculture in an era of climate change' climate risk management is an area of urgent priority. He suggested the establishment of an interdisciplinary Climate Risk Management Research and Training Centre in each of the 128 agro-climatic zones. Such centers should develop computer simulation models on various weather probabilities and develop drought, flood and good weather codes. The aim is to maximize the benefits of good seasons and minimize the damage caused by unfavorable monsoons. Prof. Swaminathan said the technology was accumulating but public policy was lagging behind. He wanted one woman and a male member of every Panchayat, chosen by the gram sabha, to be trained as 'Climate Risk Managers'. At the same time there is an urgent need for a climate response extension program. Emphasis should be on climatic information, forecasts, adoptive technology innovations and documentation and validation of ITK's in local condition perspective. Climate field schools on the pattern of Farmer field schools can also be established.

Chapter 9
AGRICULTURE CRISIS: THE WAY OUT

Agricultural situation in India needs immediate therapy. The first ever report on the state of Indian agriculture, a publication of the ministry of agriculture, government of India also depicts a fearful picture. The declining soil fertility and water availability, small size of farm holdings, low productivity of staple crops and the wastage of food grains have contributed in plunging agriculture deep in crisis. It has to be made more remunerative, land degradation has to be checked, the fragmentation of land holdings has to be stopped right now. The chapter discusses the way out to address the various issues facing the agriculture sector in India.

9.1 Diversification

An urgent shift is needed from crop centered traditional agriculture to a more diversified one. M.S. Swaminathan too calls the present conventional agriculture as an exploitative agriculture (Chaudhary, R., 2012). Rather it is an 'exploitative arrangement' which has harmed the soil, flora and fauna since long.

There are about 115 million operational holdings in the country and more than 90 per cent of these are marginal and small land holdings (Prasad, 2011). Such small land holdings besides being uneconomical hamper the use of new technology. The problem is further compounded with the presence of majority of land in rainfed areas. Farmers still concentrate on food crops such as Paddy, Wheat and Maize which are largely dependent on timely rainfall and appropriate weather conditions. For sustainable gains in agriculture, the efforts should not only be to enhance productivity but enhancing profitability, employment opportunities and enrichment of environmental and social values. All this can be achieved through diversification with allied activities like dairy, livestock, poultry, piggery, goatry, apiary, sericulture, fruit crops, mushroom cultivation, fisheries etc. The state of Kerala has a unique cropping pattern. Only 9.9 per cent of the gross cropped area is devoted to food grains as against the national average of 63.8 per cent. About 90 per cent of the area in Kerala is under high value plantation crops like condiments and species (Bhalla and Singh, 2009). The livestock based farming systems also acts as catalysts in transforming subsistence farming into income generating enterprises allowing poor households to join the market economy. Livestock has the highest effect on reducing poverty and hunger. In rural India, 43 per cent of the people who do not own even a single livestock are malnourished. Addition of one cattle or one buffalo to their assets reduces the hunger prevalence by 16 and 25 percentage points, respectively. Only 14 per cent of the people who owned one cattle and one buffalo were malnourished. Vyas (1996) and Johl (2002) also viewed that diversification to higher valued enterprises was new pathway for income growth in agriculture and rural sector. Development of suitable integrated farming system models help to realize better productivity, profitability and sustainable production systems that would help to solve the fuel, feed and energy crisis, create more employment avenues, ensure regular income and encourage agricultural oriented industry.

In developing countries the most perceived definitions of diversification is based on the assumption that it primarily involves a substitution of one crop or other agricultural product for another, or an increase in the number of enterprises, or activities, carried out by a particular farm. In the developed world, the definition relates more to the development of activities on the farm also that do not involve agricultural production. A school of thought in the British Department for Environment,

Food and Rural Affairs (DEFRA) defines diversification as "the entrepreneurial use of farm resources for a non-agricultural purpose for commercial gain". By this definition DEFRA found that 56 per cent of UK farms had diversified in 2003. The great majority of diversification activities simply involved the renting out of farm buildings for non-farming use, but 9 per cent of farms had become involved with processing or retailing, 3 per cent with provision of tourist accommodation or catering, and 7 per cent with sport or recreational activities.

9.1.1 Farming System Approach

With 2.4 per cent of the world's land India has to support 16 per cent of the world's population (Prasad and Bhatia, 2009). Indian agriculture is characterized by the predominance of marginal and small farmers. The small size of farm holdings, decrease in per capita availability of land holding, the stagnation in productivity, besides a host of other factors such as low fertility of soil, little access to modern technology, practicing traditional agricultural methods and threat of climate change looming large over the subcontinent, agriculture has become a non remunerative enterprise. Agriculture inspite of new technologies thus seems to be a losing proposition to most of the farmers. A report of the National Sample Survey Organization (Anonymous, 2005) revealed that over 40 per cent of the farmers want to leave agriculture. Even in agriculturally progressive state like Punjab 35 per cent of the farmers wants to quit their profession. There is a need to prove that farming is still a viable enterprise. This cannot be done by increasing the productivity alone. As land is limited there is no scope for horizontal expansion for food, feed and fibre production. We have to go for vertical expansion and this can be achieved through crop and enterprise diversification because no single enterprise is able to meet the ever growing food requirements of the country. Due to rapid increase in population and decrease of agricultural land no single enterprise is likely to be able to sustain the small and marginal farmers without resorting to integrated farming systems for generation of adequate income and gainful employment year round (Mahapatra, 1994). The overall agricultural scenario has to be improved with multiple goals of growth, equity, employment and efficacy. This can be done by integrating appropriate farming components requiring lesser space and time and ensuring periodic income to the farmer (Murugan and Kathiresan, 2005). An urgent shift is needed from crop centered traditional agriculture to a farming system approach. A farming system implies integration of crops and livestock with enterprises like fruit crops, fishery, goatry, poultry, and sericulture to produce more from available land, water and other resources. FAO, 2001 defines a farming system as a population of individual farm systems that have broadly similar resource base, enterprise patterns, household livelihoods and constraints and for which similar development strategies and interventions would be appropriate. The integration of different agricultural and allied enterprises with crop activity as a base provides a way to recycle low cost produces at farm level from one enterprise to another and thus reduce the cost of production and economic produce and finally to enhance the net income of the farm as a whole (Annadurai *et al.*, 1994). The development pathways include need based intensification of animal production systems, improving diversification with the appropriate mix of animals that can be mixed with the annual and perennial crops (Davendra, 2007). An estimated 500 million small farmers (both men and women) produce most of the developing world's food. Yet their families suffer from more hunger than even the urban poor, have higher rates of poverty and enjoy less access to social services. We have to meet the international commitments of halving the population of hungry and poor by 2015. This means we should reach these households. However traditional approaches have not worked. In order to provide the conditions that will permit farm households to improve their own lives governments, NGO's, and international agencies must understand more clearly the agro-ecological, physical, economic and cultural environment within which farmers and their families live *i.e.* their farming systems.

9.1.2 Drivers of Diversification

Changing Consumer Demand and Demographics

Consumer today has become aware a lot. The increasing urbanization has led to the change of consumption pattern of peoples. They are now moving away from a conventional diet based on staple food crops like rice, wheat and maize to a one with a greater content of nutrients like fruits, meat, egg, dairy etc. Such diversification from the monoculture of traditional staples can have important nutritional benefits for farmers in developing countries.

Export Potential

The different products can be obtained through diversification that have huge export potential. Farmers can successfully diversify into crops that can meet export market demand. While concern about food miles, as well as the cost of complying with supermarket certification requirements may jeopardize this success in the long run, there remains much potential to diversify to meet export markets.

Adding Value

Value addition is another concept that can raise income of the farmers. It involves adding value to the consumable items by processing them into different packaging materials so that they become ready for use and consumers have to devote less and less time to food preparation. Now in India with the entry of FDI in retail markets value addition seems to have a greater scope to raise the income of the farming community. The increased income acts as an incentive for the farmers and can drive them to diversification.

Risk

A farming system represents an appropriate combination of different enterprises in addition to crop production. The different components of farming system can be dairy, livestock, poultry, piggery, Goatry, apiary, sericulture, fruit crops, mushroom cultivation, fisheries etc. It acts as an insurance cover for the farmers as he gets compensated from other enterprise in case of failure of one enterprise. Livestock based farming systems are very important for sustainable food security. These livestock based farming systems acts as catalysts in transforming subsistence farming into income generating enterprises allowing poor households to join the market economy. The output of one component acts as an input for other enterprises. Farmers also face risk from bad weather and from fluctuating prices. Diversification offers a response to both. A diversified portfolio of products ensures that farmers do not suffer complete ruin when the market prices of certain crops fall below a certain level.

Threats both External as well as Internal

These threats arise as a result of policy changes by respective countries. The Caribbean banana industry collapsed as a result of the removal of quota protection on EU markets, making it necessary for the farmers to go for diversification. Similarly subsidies also determine to a great extent the crops that farmers will grow. Their removal or continuance provides a significant incentive for diversification. Farmers can go for a new enterprise or return to the one grown in the past depending upon the extent of subsidies. The government policy in Kenya to promote crop diversification included the removal of subsidies for some crops.

Vagaries of Weather

The vagaries of weather have become more pronounced in the recent times due to global warming and the consequent climate change. The decision of the farmers to grow the type of crops is now based on changes in temperatures and the length of the growing season. Climate change affects important parameters like water, temperature, carbon dioxide and the soil fertility status. This climate change led diversification has already been initiated by farmers in different countries like India, Canada, Srilanka, Canada, Kenya and Mozambique

Sustainability

The effective utilization of the wastes such as cow dung, litter, urine, leaves of the plants are a source of nutrients for the crops. It ultimately reduces the dependence of the farming community on the chemical fertilizers as a result of which harmful effects of the chemicals are minimized. Soil erosion is also reduced because of the planting of suitable tree species in an agro forestry system. This imparts sustainability to the system. An integrated farming system offers wide opportunities for recycling of the waste materials generated from different components of the system. The inputs can be effectively used and with greater efficiency among different enterprises.

Employment Generation

The family labour gets absorbed in performing various operations in the fields for crops as well as for other enterprises. The problem of under employment gets reduced considerably. The migration of the family members to other areas for finding out job opportunities is also minimized.

9.2 Focusing Small Farmers

Small holder farmers are defined as those marginal and sub-marginal farm households that own or/and cultivate less than 2.0 hectare of land. These constitute more than 80 percent of the total. This situation is not only confined to India but to South Asian region. Joshi *et al.* (2007) has also reported that the South Asian region despite being the second fastest growing region of the world is dominated by the small holders. This is unlike Latin America characterized by large holdings. According to Shenggen Fan, Director General of International Food Policy Research Institute small holder farms having an average size of 2 ha or less provide not only livelihoods to 2.5 billion people but also 80 per cent of the food consumed in Asia and Africa South of Sahara.

The surveys of Government of India reported that the marginal farmers having land holdings less than 1 hectare constituted 61.6 per cent of the total land holdings in 1995-96 and the small farmers having land holdings less than 2 hectares were about 18.7 per cent. Thus put together the small and marginal farmers constituted 80.3 per cent of the total in that corresponding period. In 2002-03 the percentage of such small and marginal farmers rose to 86 per cent from that of 80.3 per cent in 1995-96 (Agrawal, 2012). These farmers cultivate mainly low value, subsistence crops and have lower productivity since the farmer's practice subsistence farming without the generation of any surplus. The farmers have low income level and are still out of reach of modern technological knowhow. According to a World Bank report, as much as 87 per cent of marginal and 70 per cent of small farmers do not get credit through institutions (Rao, 2010). For these marginal and small farmers economic viability of farming is a big issue.

What is more serious that various policies of the government like acquiring land for Special Economic Zones are pushing these marginal and small farmers out of agriculture. This group is still largely outside the reach of the technological interventions. This has also been reported by Bunch (1982) who suggested that the gap between agricultural research, and the developing nation's small-scale, resource poor farmer has been increasing due to a decline in the technology generated which can actually be put to practical use by the poor farmer. Shanner, Philipp, and Schmehl

(1982) have reported that, farmers with limited resources often do not adopt new technologies because their conditions are not like those where the technologies were developed, they do not have resources to purchase the required inputs, the technologies do not apply to the crops grown or the livestock raised on their farms or the way they operate, or they do not know about the new technologies".

The 11th Five Year Plan had also stressed that the agricultural strategy must focus on 85 per cent of farmers who are small and marginal, increasingly female and who find it difficult to access inputs, credit and extension or to market their output. While some of these farmers may ultimately exit from farming, the overwhelming majority will continue to remain in the sector and the objective of inclusiveness requires that their needs are attended to. Small and marginal farms are not uneconomical. They can be made more bio diverse by doing away with monocultures. Infact studies have revealed that small biodiverse farms have higher productivity than monocultures. Let me take an example of Pearl Millet from Rajasthan. The monocultures of Pearl Millet gave a per ace net profit of Rupees 2480, whereas a biodiverse farm of Pearl Millet, Moth Bean and Sesame gave a per acre net profit of Rupees 12045. Similarly in Uttaranchal, a monoculture of paddy gave a per acre return of Rupees 6720 per acre, whereas a biodiverse farm gave a return of Rupees 24,600 per acre. There is a vast scope for small farms in India. Their productivity can be increased by conserving the natural resources. On the other hand the large farms are chemical intensive and it has been found that the chemical farming needs ten times more water than ecological farming and this also makes the climate unstable. Water is also over exploited in such type of farms and biodiversity is also lost. As such small biodiverse farms based on internal inputs are in fact the only promise for increasing agricultural productivity. Indian agro-climatic regional planning has documented the zones of maximal opportunity for diversified agriculture on smaller farms. This can be utilized to plan for such small farms so that they can be made more profitable and ecologically safe. The National Commission for Enterprises in the Unorganized Sector (NCEUS) has also recommended a special programme for marginal and small farmers. Infact a report of NCEUS analyzed the status and constraints faced by marginal and small farmers. It focused on the need for a special programme which aimed at capacity building of these farmers in both the farm and non-farm activities. The report said that the marginal and small farmers suffer from market failures in agriculture in terms of credit, supply of inputs, marketing of output and access to new technologies etc. NCUS thus recommended measures like Special programmes for marginal and small farmers; Emphasis on accelerated land and water management; credit for marginal and small farmers and a Farmers' debt relief commission. The Commission also strongly advocated that a strategy for marginal and small farmers must focus on group approaches like the Co-operatives, the Producer's Companies, the Farmers' groups and SEWA (Self Employed Women's Association) like Farmers' model. The Director General of International Food Research Institute Shenngen Fan also illustrated how linking of farmers with dairy grid in India connected over 13 million of farmers and what is inspiring is that of this 13 million, 25 per cent are women. This has increased their bargaining power besides providing timely information.

Quoting late Prime minister of India Choudhary Charan Singh who said, "Agriculture being a life process, in actual practice under given conditions, yields per acre decline as the size of the farm increases and the output per acre of investment is higher on small farms than on large farms. If a crowded, capital-scarce country like India has a choice between a single 100 acre farm and forty 2.5 acre farms, the capital cost to the national economy will be less if a country chooses the small farms.

9.3 Doing away with Yield Gaps

The National Commission on Farmers indicated a technology fatigue in Indian agriculture and a large knowledge gap between the yields in research stations and actual yields in farmers' fields. The yield gaps given by the Planning Commission (2007) on the basis of 2003-05 data were very large gaps. In case of Wheat the yield gap varied from 6 per cent in Punjab to 84 per cent in Madhya Pradesh; in rice it was over 100 per cent in Assam, Bihar, Chattisgarh and UP; in maize: it ranged from 7 per cent in Gujarat to 300 per cent in Assam; in Jowar it varied from 13 per cent in Madhya Pradesh to 200 per cent in Karnataka; in mustard, it was 5 per cent in Haryana to 150 per cent in Chattisgarh. Similarly in case of Soybean, the yield gap was 7 per cent in Rajasthan to 185 per cent in

Karnataka and in case of Sugarcane it varied from 16 per cent in Andhra Pradesh to 167 per cent.

States like Bihar, Orissa, Assam, West Bengal and Uttar Pradesh are the states in which current yield levels are below the national average yield. These states account for 66 per cent of rice area and need immediate emphasis on bridging yield gaps to attain target demand and yield growth. For wheat we must focus mainly on Uttar Pradesh, Madhya Pradesh, Bihar and Rajasthan accounting for 68 per cent of wheat area. For coarse cereals, major emphasis must be given to Rajasthan, Maharashtra, Karnataka, Madhya Pradesh, Andhra Pradesh and Uttar Pradesh. To meet the demand for pulses greater emphasis is needed in almost all the states with particular focus on Madhya Pradesh, Maharashtra, Rajasthan, Gujarat, Andhra Pradesh, Karnataka and Uttar Pradesh which have three-fourths of total area under pulses cultivation. In cases of oilseeds the focus should be on states like Andhra Pradesh, Madhya Pradesh, Rajasthan, Maharashtra, Karnataka, West Bengal and Uttar Pradesh to increase the yield by about 4 per cent.

9.4 Cropping Intensity

The area under crops can grow either through increase in net area sown or through increase in the intensity of cultivation. Since a limit has been reached with regard to the possibility of increasing net sown area on a substantial scale, the only method of increasing GCA is by increasing cropping intensity through bringing more area under irrigation or by the introduction of short duration varieties. Cropping intensity *i.e.* gross sown area as per cent of net sown area increased from 111 per cent in 1950-51 to 115 per cent in 1960-61, 118 per cent in 1970—71 and 130 per cent by mid 1990s. Presently it is 138 per cent which means it can be further increased by bringing more and more area under irrigation and farm mechanization.

9.5 Use of Modern Inputs

There is a clear association between levels of land productivity and the use of modern inputs. A high correlation between the quantum and intensity of inputs used and yield levels across states has confirmed the role of inputs in raising yields. All the high productivity in states like

Punjab, Haryana, Kerala, Tamilnadu and Gujarat could be attributed to use of modern inputs. On the other side the use of input in states like Rajasthan, Madhya Pradesh, Orissa, Maharashtra was abysmally low. Compared with 412 kg per hectare of fertilizer used in Punjab during the period 2003-06 the use of fertilizers was just 58 kg, 61 kg, 80 kg and 94 kg per hectare in Rajasthan, Orissa, Madhya Pradesh and Maharashtra respectively and the situation holds for other inputs also (Bhalla and Singh, 2009). One of the important questions that is raised is whether it is sustainable in the long run to maintain the tempo of agriculture in the country by the use of costly and heavily subsidized inputs that not only pose a heavy fiscal burden but also lead to soil and water conservation.

9.6 Farm Mechanization

Mechanization has immense importance in multiple cropping and diversification of agriculture. It enables efficient utilization of inputs such as seeds, fertilizers and irrigation water. It has been revealed that with suitable engineering interventions it is possible to decrease the cost of cultivation by 20 per cent and increase the productivity by 15 per cent (Kumar, 2012). Farm mechanization in the country has been low as compared to countries like China, Thailand, Korea.

Table 28: Effect of Mechanization on different Aspects of Crop Production

Aspect of Mechanization	*Percentage Increase*
Increase in productivity	12-34
Seed cum fertilizer drill results in	
Savings in seeds	20
Savings in fertilizers	15-20
Enhancement in cropping intensity	5-22
Increase in gross income of farmers	29-49

Source: Report of the Sub-Group on Agricultural Implements and Machinery, formulated for 9th Five Year Plan, Government of India.

Singh and Singh (1972) in their study came out with the conclusion that tractor farms gave higher yields of wheat, Paddy and Sugarcane and produced a higher overall gross output per hectare than non tractor farms. The average increase of productivity on farms hiring tractors was reported to be 11.8 per cent, 13.0 per cent and 16.0 per cent for paddy, sugarcane and groundnut respectively. The sowing of wheat in Northern plains including Punjab, Haryana is done by the first fortnight of November. A delay beyond this period by one week leads to about 1.50 quintals per acre decrease in the yield. This is true for other crops also and for other farm operations like hoeing, weeding, threshing which need to be performed at the right time otherwise the yields and the incomes are affected severely. A significant increase in cropping intensity has been reported due to the use of tractors and irrigation as a consequence of mechanization. The increase in cropping intensity has been reported to be 165, 156 and 149 per cent respectively for tractor-owning, tractor using and bullock operated farms respectively, according to a NCAER (1980) survey. Similar results have been reported in other studies which have concluded that as a consequence of mechanization, the cropping intensity increased significantly. Singh (2001) concluded that cropping intensity was mainly dependent on annual water availability and the farm power available. He reported that the States like Punjab, Haryana, and Uttar Pradesh which had higher per cent irrigated area, higher doses of fertilizer and higher power availability per hectare also had higher grain yield per hectare. The Agriculture engineering scientist should develop tools for timeliness of farm operations, drudgery reduction and efficient input use. The impact of farm mechanization on labour employment has always been a cause of concern. Not much emperical evidences are made but the study of Rao and Singh (1964) on Tractorisation in Kanjhawala block in Delhi territory" revealed that both tractor as well as non tractor farms had on an average 8.2 person per farm and the labour surplus at their farm was neither surplus nor adequate. GIPE Poona (1967) also revealed that Tractorisation generated greater demand for labour by facilitating more intense cultivation. Further other studies have also came to the conclusion that the net human labour displacement in agricultural operations gets compensated by multiple cropping, greater intensity of cultivation and higher yields. Farm mechanization also indirectly provides employment to skilled and unskilled persons who are engaged in operation, repair and maintenance of prime movers and farm equipment. NCAER (1980) also revealed that tractorized farms reduced their draught animal stock and increased their milch.

The department of Agriculture and Cooperation also aims to promote an integrated National mission on Agricultural mechanization. This mission aims to put the small and marginal farmers at the core of intervention with a special emphasis on reaching the unreached.

It will lay emphasis on bringing farm mechanization to those villages where technologies employed are decades old. At the same time there is a need to promote human resource development in the field of agriculture mechanization, adequate financial assistance and subsidy for procuring farm implements, establishing farm machinery banks and using appropriate media to create awareness among the farming community regarding these implements.

9.7 Augmenting Irrigation Capacity

India possesses 16 per cent of the world's population but just 4 per cent of its water resources. Of the 182.70 million hectares of land used for cultivation only about 62 million hectares is currently irrigated (Gautam and Sapheia, 2011). India receives an average of 4,000 billion cubic meters of rainfall every year and only 48 per cent of rainfall ends in Indian rivers. Due to lack of storage and crumbling infrastructure, only 18 per cent can be utilized. Total water consumption is expected to rise by 20-40 per cent over the next 20 years. India is not poor in water resources. What it lacks is the ability to efficiently capture and effectively utilize the available resources for maximum benefit. The current water use efficiency of the canal irrigation is the lowest. It is 35 per cent which is lowest in the world. Water shed development and rainwater harvesting are of course a focus area for sustainable agricultural production. Even if 5 per cent of the annual rainfall were harvested properly, that will produce a substantial quantum of water to the tune of 900 million litres. Proposals to link some of the major rivers together could channel surpluses from flood prone areas into drought-prone regions, create millions of hectares of additional irrigated land, provide an inexpensive system of inland water transport, and generate millions of additional employment opportunities in construction, agriculture, trade and industrial development. At the same time attention should be paid for the efficient management of available water resources. In Australia water consumption in agriculture has been reduced by 30 per cent in the last 20 years by good agricultural practices.

9.8 Increasing Water Use Efficiency

Paucity of water for irrigation is to be the biggest challenge for agricultural sector. About 92 per cent of the ground water extracted is used in the agriculture sector, 5 and 3 per cent are used for industrial and domestic sectors in India respectively (Awais and Zaidi, 2010). To produce one kilogram of rice Punjab consumes 5400 litres of water whereas West Bengal needs only 2400 litres of water. It has been rightly said that the production now needs to be measured by per thousand litres of water used for irrigation and not by yields per hectare. Since independence, India has built a formidable irrigation infrastructure.

Though India has the second largest irrigated area in the world, the area under assured irrigation or at least minimal drainage is not adequate. It is estimated that 10 per cent increase in water use efficiency can bring an additional 14 million hectares under irrigated cultivation (Kumar, K. 2010). Even with 20 per cent of the irrigation intensity, there is a sharp fall in the proportion of hunger and poverty and it remains there irrespective of further intensification of irrigation. Evidences suggest that extensive irrigation will prove much more effective than to adding more and more water, and often wasting it along with the associated degradation of the natural resources. Such a policy will not only reduce poverty and hunger, but will also promote equity and environmental protection and natural resource conservation. In the context of managing this scant resource effectively, micro irrigation technologies are useful in raising productivity, increasing farm incomes through crop yields and outputs. Drip irrigation saves 25-60 per cent of water whereas sprinklers save 25-33 per cent of water

9.9 Food Processing

The industry is estimated to be worth around US $ 67 billion and employing about 13 million people directly and about 35 million people indirectly. According to the CII, the food processing sector has the potential of attracting $ 33 billion of investment in 10 years besides generating employment for 9 million men days. The Indian food processing industry is currently growing at 13 per cent compounded annual growth rate and is rightly described by former Prime minister Dr. Manmohan Singh as the sunrise sector. With a huge production base, India can easily become one of the leading food suppliers to the world while at the same time serving the vast growing domestic market of over a billion people. India's large market size with growing incomes and changing life styles also create incredible market opportunities for food producers, food processors, machinery makers, food technologists and service providers in this sector. The right post harvest practices such as good processing techniques, and proper packaging, transportation and storage (of even processed foods) can play a significant role in reducing spoilage and extending shelf life. Food processing benefits all the sections of the society. It helps the farmers to have higher yield, better revenues and lower the risks drastically, Consumers have access to a greater variety, better prices and new products. Ultimately the economy also gets benefitted with new business opportunities for the entrepreneurs and the work force gets employment.

9.10 Preventing Grain Drain

Given the loopholes in the existing Public Distribution System, the use of food stamps as is already in practice in countries like US can also be tried in India. Under this scheme the intended beneficiaries are provide with food stamps which recipients can exchange for an equivalent amount of food grains at any shop. The shopkeepers can get them credited into their bank accounts. To avoid the rotting of food grains in the open community grain storage banks should be established at the village or Panchayat level from which the peoples could get food at subsidized rates. Andhra Pradesh has started issuing coupons for rice and Kerosene under Targeted Public Distribution System to ensure that there is no impersonation or false accounting in distribution of essential commodities by fair price shop dealers. Coupons are issued to the beneficiaries at the time of issuance or renewal of ration cards. The next month's allocation is based on the coupons submitted to the fair price shop dealer. A chapter has already been devoted to the Public Distribution system in the book.

9.11 Utilizing Wasteland

The National Wasteland Development Board defines wasteland as degraded land which can be brought under vegetative cover, with reasonable effort and which is currently lying unutilized and land which is deteriorating for lack of appropriate water and soil management or on account of natural cause. In India about 43 million hectares of waste land can be utilized effectively to contribute significantly in meeting the food, energy and other requirements of the country besiding creating employment opportunities for rural landless population of the area. Plantations of fast-growing trees such as *Casurina equistifolia*, Jotropha can help to generate thousands of megawatts of power from renewable, forest-based fuel sources in a cost-effective manner. This would reduce India's dependence on imported fuel oils which are under the threat of being getting extinct. It is estimated that two hectares of cultivated wasteland can generate an annual net income ranging from approximately Rs 15,000-50,000 and year-round employment for one person. Casurina is being commercially cultivated as a rainfed crop in the southern states of Tamil Nadu. It has multiple uses like fuel, construction and paper making and has a high calorific value of 3500 kilo calories. The environmental benefits of the plant include control of erosion and reclamation of poor soils. One hectare of Casurina under rainfed conditions can produce on average 40 to 50 tons of fuel per annum. Similarly Prosopis grows wild on extensive areas of wasteland ranging from sandy, loamy, sodic, saline, alkaline and marshy soils with very little input and at very low cost. Its biomass is an excellent raw material for power generation. The wood is hardy with calorific value more than that from coal. Each hectare of Prosopis creates 100 man-days of labour per annum.

9.12 Agriculture Infrastructure

A London based think tank, Economist Intelligence Unit (EIU), sponsored by US Corporation Du Point on September 26, 2013 released the Global Food Security Index (GFSI, 2012) in which among 105 nations India ranked at 66th which is a moderate position. The index measures the nations that are most and least vulnerable to food insecurity, using 25 indicators divided into three categories: affordability and financial access; availability and utilization called quality and safety. India scored moderately in the overall index and across all three categories viz affordability, availability and utilization. Of the three categories, India scored highest in food availability as 51.3 per cent, but lowest in food affordability as 38.4 per cent which indicates poor access to food grains because of infrastructure problems. The nutritional quality and safety was ranked 44.2 per cent.

What we are lacking is good post harvest infrastructure. Lack of good infrastructure is holding India back. A recent statement of then minister of Agriculture in the Rajya Sabha confirmed the loss due to lack of inadequate infrastructure to the tune of rupees 44,000 crore. Of this the value of annual wastage of fruits and vegetables was estimated at rupees 13,309 crore. The Saumitra Chaudhari committee constituted by the planning commission in 2012 had put the total cold storage capacity requirements in the country at 61.3 million tonnes as against the present annual capacity of around 29 million tonnes. There is thus a gap of 32 million tonnes. The government provides financial assistance in the form of grant in aid at the rate of 50 per cent of the total cost of plants and machinery and technical civil works in general areas and at the rate of 75 per cent in difficult areas including north eastern states for creation of cold chain infrastructure with a ceiling of rupees 10 crore. The government has also formulated a scheme called as PEG for creation of additional storage capacity for guaranteed hiring by the Food Corporation of India. In this scheme against a target of 60 lakh tonne capacity creation in the year 2013-14, 3.36 lakh was completed up to July 2013. Today in India cold storage facility is used only for ten per cent of the produce and over 3500 of existing cold storage warehouses have only around 13 million tonnes of storage capacity.

The Governrnent of India has also already taken some initiatives for safety of farm produce. India's first horticulture train started operation in June 2012 this year carrying onions from Nasik farmers to Kolkata. This has proved very successful for small farmers who do not have to become victim of middlemen and commission agents. This horticulture express will deliver consignments to Chitpur near Kolkata covering 1800 km in 36 hours. Currently onions are transported by Trucks that need 120 hours for the journey. The train has been jointly introduced by the National Horticultural Board and the container corporation of Railways. The government has also started setting up of National Center for Cold Chain development in the wake of mounting post harvest losses. As many as 39 cold chain projects were approved during 2011. Ten mega food parks have been approved in Andhra Pradesh, Punjab, Jharkhand, Assam, West Bengal, Uttrakhand, Tamil Nadu, Karnataka, Bihar and Tripura. These Mega Food Parks are aimed at accelerating the pace of food processing in the country backed by an efficient food supply chain. Besides this the parks will provide employment opportunities for so many peoples.

Most of the perishable items are produced in the villages which remain confined to these areas due to the absence of road networks The existing road and rail facilities are inadequate. Most of the areas which produce good quality fruits are still inaccessible. This coupled with the rough terrain of the area and lack of regulatory markets make the farming community to suffer a lot at the hands of the local traders. Farmers have no information about the market price. There is an urgent need to establish suitable infrastructure like the use of information communication technology (ICT) for benefit of farming community. The technology like e-kiosks and e-choupals of Indian Tobacco Company in Madhya Pradesh and other states of the country are doing a great job. Each electronic kiosk is connected to a number of villages. The villagers can obtain any information easily from these kiosks regarding various aspects of crop production. Communication with different markets and among different stakeholders is also possible through the use of ICT.

Irrigation is another area which requires infrastructure up gradation. With suitable infrastructure the irrigation potential can be increased. The utilization of available water for agriculture too is far from efficient. Wastage of water is huge in surface irrigation systems. The inability to conserve adequate water and curb its indiscriminate utilization, including rampant wasteful exploitation of water is also a cause of concern. The problem is more severe in dry land area of the country which account for more than 60 per cent of the total cultivable area. Suitable water conserving infrastructure like the Drip irrigation and sprinkler irrigation should be installed in these areas. Water conservation techniques like water sheds, rainwater harvesting and other measures can bring additional area under irrigation in these water scarce regions. Solar energy is also another area which can be exploited for use in agriculture. For this solar panels should be provided to the farmers or the government should take the initiative. The Gujarat government has started laying solar panels on irrigation channels like canals. These panels generate energy for various agricultural operations as well as control loss of water by preventing water erosion as the water channels are covered with solar panels. The solar energy has the advantage of being a renewable source, with no pollution and no green house gas emission thus making agriculture sustainable in the long run.

The than Finance minister and now President of India, Shri Pranab Mukherjee and our Ex Prime Minister, Dr. Manmohan Singh, have also appealed states to appeal bigger industries to invest in developing infrastructure of agricultural supply chain. Moreover, the government has emphasized on increasing investments of private sector in marketing, transportation and storage facility of fast degradable agricultural products. The private sector should also come forward and invest in creating agriculture assets. They can use it on a built operate transfer basis.

At the same time greater emphasis has to be laid on research infrastructure by establishing a number of new institutes, national research centers for several crops and livestock to address the local problems and come out with site specific solutions. We have to go for pro-active policy on storage of agricultural produce to address this problem along with emphasis on research and development, multi-crop system and better land and water management and providing road or rail connectivity to the areas which are still outside the connectivity network. The steering committee on Agriculture for the eleventh five year plan in its report said that, 'Agriculture markets are still underdeveloped and in several cases farmers do not receive the remunerative prices. There are no arrangements for procurement at support prices for many of the crops other than wheat and Paddy at many places in the country. The rural areas are not still penetrated by the markets. On an average a rural market serves an area of one hundred sixteen square kilometer instead of eighty square kilometer as proposed by National Farmers commission (Minocha, N. 2012). Rural roads are the route to farm efficiency. The development of all weather roads facilitates a shift from traditional agriculture to off season crops and horticulture. A report of the Planning commission's Programme Evaluation Organization based on the study conducted in seven states revealed that farmer's income increased by 17.66 per cent in the states collectively, where infrastructure was available. Similarly the construction of a bridge over river Mahanadi in Jagat Singh Pura in Orissa connected 80 villages with four strategic markets and the bridge also resulted in diversification and mechanization of agriculture. Similarly an Asian Development Bank report in 2010 also highlighted that the rural roads resulted in 20 per cent increase in visits by farmers to nearby markets and 13 per cent decrease in incidence of agricultural produce getting spoiled or damaged in transit. An IFPRI study said that enhanced returns from agricultural production could be obtained by agricultural production by giving more thrust to agricultural research and development (13.45 per cent), roads (5.31 per cent), education (1.39 per cent) soil and water conservation (0.96 per cent).

9.13 Genetically Modified Crops

Much is talked of about the genetically modified crops. The protagonist of the GM crops say that for ensuring food security of burgeoning world population genetically modified crops are must. In the next 50 years the global population is expected to double, reaching more than 8 billion people by 2050. As such the world food supply has to be increased drastically. The amount of land currently committed to food production cannot yield the amount of food needed by this increased population. We can ill afford to clear forests to increase acreage, Therefore a better approach is to find ways of getting greater crop yield from existing land. Genetic engineering is much talked about approach to increase the quantity of the harvest. While one view is that Genetic engineering can address the factors that traditionally deplete crops such as pests, weeds, drought and wind and the genetically modified plants can deal with these hardships and dramatically increase the percentage of crops that survive and are harvested each year. But those who oppose the genetically modified crops have their own logic. They have doubts regarding the safety, regulation and negative impact on the environment. The debate has indeed assumed alarming dimensions.

Before going ahead let me discuss what genetically modified crops are. The term GM foods or GMOs (genetically-modified organisms) is most commonly used to refer to crop plants created for human or animal consumption using the latest molecular biology techniques. These plants have been modified in the laboratory to enhance desired traits such as increased resistance to herbicides or improved nutritional content. Genetic modification involves altering an organism's DNA. This can be done by altering an existing section of DNA or by adding a new gene altogether. The enhancement of desired traits has traditionally been undertaken through breeding but conventional plant breeding methods can be very time consuming and are often not very accurate. Genetic engineering, on the other hand, can create plants with the exact desired trait very rapidly and with great accuracy. For example, plant geneticists can isolate a gene responsible for drought tolerance and insert that gene into a different plant. The new genetically-modified plant will gain drought tolerance as well. Not only can genes be transferred from one plant to another, but genes from non-plant organisms also can be used. The best known example of this is the use of Bt genes in corn and other crops. Bt or *Bacillus thuringiensis* is a naturally occurring bacterium that produces crystal proteins that are lethal to insect larvae. A gene is a code that governs how we appear and what characteristics we have. When a crop is genetically modified a foreign gene is inserted in the plant's own genes.

This might be a gene from a bacterium resistant to pesticide or an anti freeze gene resistant to severe cold. Let us take another example, a frost resistant tomato plant has been developed by adding an antifreeze gene from a coldwater fish to it. The antifreeze gene comes from the coldwater flounder, a fish that can survive in very cold conditions. The result is that the plant receives the characteristics held within the genetic code. Consequently, the genetically modified plant also becomes able to withstand frost. The GM tomato plant contains a copy of the flounder antifreeze gene in every one of its cells. The plant is tested to see if the fish gene still works. The plant developed is resistant to frost. With genetic modification it is possible to transfer genes from one species to another. This is because all genes, be they human, plant, animal or bacterial are created from the same material. Genetic scientists therefore have a huge amount of genetic characteristics to choose from.

GM foods promise to meet this need in a number of ways. Growing GM foods such as Bt corn can help eliminate the application of chemical pesticides and reduce the cost of bringing a crop to market. Crop plants to be resistant to one very powerful herbicide could help prevent environmental damage by reducing the amount of herbicides needed. For example, Monsanto has created a strain of soybeans genetically modified to be not affected by their herbicide product Roundup. A farmer grows these soybeans which then only require one application of instead of multiple applications, reducing production cost and limiting the dangers of agricultural waste run-off. Creating plants that can withstand long periods of drought or high salt content in soil and groundwater will help people to grow crops in formerly inhospitable place. Malnutrition is common in third world countries where impoverished peoples rely on a single crop such as rice for the main staple of their diet. However, rice does not contain adequate amounts of all necessary nutrients to prevent malnutrition. If rice could be genetically engineered to contain additional vitamins and minerals, nutrient deficiencies could be alleviated. For example, blindness due to vitamin A deficiency is a common problem in third world countries. Researchers at the Swiss Federal Institute of Technology Institute for Plant Sciences have created a strain of "golden" rice containing an unusually high content of beta-carotene (vitamin A).

9.13.1 The Issue of Genetic Modification

But the other side of the coin is that is it ethical to insert a gene from a fish in the tomato. By doing this are not we changing vegetarians to non vegetarians. There have been reports where serious doubts have been raised about the reliability of tests conducted on crops raised by Genetic modifications. Further the private players like Monsanto which are actively propagating GM crops, would they label their products with the ingredients of which the products are made. After all in a democratic set up, it is every one's right to know what product he is eating. It is also said that the long term effects of foods developed using biotechnology are unknown. A report of the Punjab and Haryana unit of Rashtriya Kisan Sangthan based on the feedback they received from Bt Cotton growers of Malwa Belt of Punjab at Bathinda must serve as an eye opener. Nearly 95 per cent of the participants in the meeting agreed to the fact that their per acre yield in Bt Cotton have been declining since 2011 especially after the introduction of Bt Cotton (Gene 2). The prime factor reported to be responsible for this decline was attack of White Fly on Bt cotton. The report further said that it seems that the romantic era of farmers with Bt Cotton is on verge of end because the seed companies rather than addressing the contemporary issues of Bt growers are showcasing a few handpicked success stories of Bt Cotton. A host of regulatory authorities including the

United States Department of Agriculture and the US Environmental Protection Agency have determined that these products are safe to introduce into the food supply. While there is no such thing as "zero risk" for any food, consumers can be confident that foods produced using biotechnology meet the same stringent safety standards as foods producing using conventional methods.

Genetically modified (GM) foods have continued to be a source of scrutiny and heated debate, and in 2013 countries continued to adopt different approaches to GM foods and the related issue of bio safety. For example, Mexico introduced an indefinite ban on genetically engineered corn, whereas Bangladesh approved the commercial cultivation of GM eggplant that is resistant to insect damage. In the Philippines, field trials of GM rice (often dubbed golden rice) were vandalized. Still there are interrogative sentences in the mind of a common man which need to be addressed before taking a final decision on the issue. Let us all hope that the regulatory mechanism in India like the Genetic Engineering Approval Committee looks into all these aspects

9.14 Crop Insurance

Agriculture in India is subjected to various risks and uncertainties. While uncertainty refers to an event the outcome of which is not certain *i.e.* the outcome may be one of the many possible outcomes, Risk on the other hand refers to the impact of the uncertain outcome on the quantity or value of some economic variable. The value of the economic variable may be on either side of the mean value. Thus risk refers to the variations in value of an economic variable resulting from the influence of an uncertain event. Since the variations in the value are measurable, risk can be measured (Singh, Gurdev 2010). Some of these risks are human made while some are as a result of natural phenomenon. The man made risks are as a result of fire, indiscriminate use of fertilizers, pesticides and other chemicals, price risks, etc whereas the natural disasters are from the climate extremes like the unprecedented rains resulting in floods or sometimes the lack of rainfall resulting in drought like conditions. In India the annual rainfall distribution pattern is highly uneven; 74 per cent from South West Monsoon (June -Sept) 13 per cent from Pre Monsoon (Mar to May) 10 per cent from North East Monsoon (Oct to Dec.) and 3 per cent in winter (Jan

- Feb). This huge variation thus makes agriculture in India prone to the vagaries of weather. The need to protect farmers from vulnerability both natural as well as manmade has been a continuing concern of agricultural policy. The National Agriculture Policy 2000 states "Despite technological and economic advancements, the condition of farmers continues to be unstable due to natural calamities and price fluctuations".

All these events severely affect the farmers through loss in production and farm income, and they are beyond the control of the farmers. With the weather becoming quiet unpredictable the loss due to the natural disasters is increasing in frequency as well as magnitude. The question is how to protect farmers by minimizing such losses. The government of India announces the Minimum Support Prices (MSP) for certain crops. The MSP is intended to provide a means of financial security to the farming community so that the farmers do not sell their produce at a rate below the MSP declared by the government. But most of the crops and in most of the states the MSP is not implemented strictly. The lack of procurement facilities accompanied by the chain of middlemen ultimately force the farmers to sell their produce sometimes at a throw away prices. In recent times, mechanisms like contract farming and futures trading have been established which are expected to provide some insurance against price fluctuations directly or indirectly.

Crop insurance is considered an important and effective mechanism to address the various risks associated with crop production from various natural and manmade events. It is one method by which farmers can stabilize farm income and investment and guard against disastrous effect of losses due to natural hazards or low market prices. Agricultural insurance not only stabilizes the farm income but also helps the farmers to initiate production activity after a bad agricultural year. It cushions the shock of crop losses by providing farmers with a minimum amount of protection. Agriculture insurance forms an important component of safety-net programmes and is also being experienced in many developed countries like USA and Canada as well as in the European Union. Unfortunately, agricultural insurance in the country has not made much headway even though the need to protect Indian farmers from agriculture variability has been a continuing concern of agriculture policy.

There are two major categories of agricultural insurance: single and multi-peril coverage. Single peril coverage offers protection from single hazard while multi-peril provides protection from several hazards. In India, multi-peril crop insurance programme is being implemented, considering the overwhelming impact of nature on agricultural output and its disastrous consequences on the society, in general, and farmers, in particular. It is also important to mention that crop insurance is based on either Area approach or Individual approach. The claims are paid to the credit institutions in the case of loanee farmers and to the individuals who insured their crops in the other cases. The credit institution adjust the amount against the crop loan and pay the residual amount, if any, to the farmer. In the case of individual approach, assessment of loss is made separately for each insured farmer. It could be for each plot or for the farm as a whole (consisting of more than one plot at different locations). Individual farm based insurance is suitable for high-value crops grown under standard practices. Liability is than limited to cost of cultivation. This type of insurance provides for accurate and timely compensation. However, it involves high administrative costs.

The history of crop insurance can be traced back to sixties when the government of India, ministry of agriculture circulated a draft proposal among the states regarding the crop insurance. The proposal did not got favour of states due to the paucity of funds. But, Punjab government sent a proposal requesting financial assistance from the government of India. This made the basis of crop insurance in India. The Government of India experimented with a comprehensive crop insurance scheme which failed. The Government later on introduced in 1999-2000, a new scheme, National Agricultural Insurance Scheme (NAIS) or Rashtriya Krishi Bima Yojana (RKBY). It covers all farmers, both loanees and non-loanees, under the scheme. The National Agricultural Insurance Scheme (NAIS) aims to provide insurance coverage and financial support to the farmers in the event of failure of any of the notified crop as a result of natural calamities, pests and diseases. The scheme covers food crops (Cereals, Millets and Pulses), Oilseeds, Sugarcane, Cotton and Potato (Annual Commercial/ annual Horticultural crops). The risks covered include yield losses due to non preventable risks, Natural Fire and Lightning Storm, Hailstorm, Cyclone, Typhoon, Tempest, Hurricane, Tornado etc. Flood, Inundation and Landslide Drought, Dry spells Pests/Diseases etc. Losses arising out of war and nuclear risks, malicious damage and other preventable risks are however excluded. Similarly the weather based insurance scheme is the largest weather based insurance scheme in the world covering 12 million farmers and presently implemented in 16 states across the country.

Agricultural Insurance Company of India Ltd (AIC) which was incorporated in December, 2002, and started operating from April, 2003, took over the implementation of NAIS. This scheme is available to both loanees and non-loanees. Recently some other insurance schemes have also come into operation in the country which go beyond yield loss and also cover the non- crop sector. These include Farm Income Insurance Scheme, Rainfall Insurance Scheme and Livestock Insurance Scheme. The Livestock insurance is provided by public sector insurance companies and the insurance cover is available for almost all livestock species. Normally, an animal is insured up to 100 per cent of the market value.

The Weather Based Crop Insurance/Rainfall Insurance scheme was started during the year 2003-04 when the private sector came out with some insurance products in agriculture based on weather parameters. The ICICI-Lombard General Insurance Company developed Rainfall insurance. This move was followed by IFFCO-Tokio General Insurance Company and by public sector Agricultural Insurance Company of India (AIC). Under the scheme, coverage for deviation in the rainfall index is extended and compensations for economic losses due to less or more than normal rainfall are paid. ICICI Lombard, World Bank and the Social Initiatives Group (SIG) of ICICI Bank collaborated in the design and pilot testing of India's first Index based Weather Insurance product in 2003-04 which covered 200 groundnut and castor farmers in the rain-fed district of Mehaboobnagar, Andhra Pradesh. Weather Based Crop Insurance Scheme (WBCIS) is also a unique weather based insurance product designed to provide insurance protection against losses in crop yield resulting from adverse weather incidences. It provides payout against adverse rainfall incidence (both deficit and excess) during kharif and adverse incidence in weather parameters like frost, heat, relative humidity, un-seasonal rainfall etc., during rabi. It operates on the concept of area approach *i.e.*, for the purpose of compensation, a reference unit area shall be linked to a reference weather station on the basis of which weather data and claims would be processed. This scheme is available to both loanees (compulsory) and non-loanees (voluntary). In India more than eighty per cent of the farmers are outside the ambit of agricultural insurance. Most of the farmers are illiterate and do not understand the procedural and other requirements of formal financial institutions and, therefore, shy away from them. It is high time the authorities should increase the awareness of the farmers regarding the insurance schemes and simplify the procedure.

There is no doubt that the government of India has launched various schemes for covering various agricultural crops but agriculture insurance has served very limited purpose. The coverage through insurance schemes in terms of area under crops, number of farmers is still very less. Statistics reveal that in the country only 25 million out of a total of 120 million farmers are under crop insurance and 90 per cent farmers are loanee farmers. The government of India has targeted to double the number of farmers from 25 to 50 million in the twelfth five year plan.

Raju and Chand have also given some policy suggestions. They argued that as Banks also benefit from the Crop Insurance Schemes, an arrangement like that in Philippines can be tried in the country. In that country banks have to share a part of the premium. For rice where the premium is 10.81 per cent, borrowing farmer pays only 2.91 per cent, the government share is 5.90 per cent and the lending institution share is 2 per cent. Such type of arrangement can be recommended for banks in India and more non loanee farmers can be brought into the fold of banking network. Private sector participation in agriculture insurance can be encouraged. Only two companies in the private sector have initiated crop insurance and that too on a small scale. ICICI-Lombard was the first company to experiment with rainfall insurance in 2003. As the insurance through government agencies has not been able to cross 15 per cent, involving private sector can enhance the coverage. Insurance should also be provided by seed companies so that farmers who paid high prices for seeds such as GM crops did not suffer in case of crop failure.

9.15 Promoting Agri-Tourism

The Tourism sector in India contributes more than 5 per cent of India's GDP with more than 350 million domestic tourists and about 3.92 million international tourists arriving in India. The Forex earnings from this industry are to the tune of 25,000 crores. It also provides 38.8 million direct and indirect jobs. The demand for travel and tourism in India is expected to grow by 8.2 per cent between 2010 and 2019 and will place India at the third position in the world. India's travel and tourism sector is expected to be the second largest employer in the world, employing 4,0037,000 by 2019.

Now a day's agri tourism is given a lot of importance. Agri Tourism is defined as travel, which combines agricultural or rural settings with products of agricultural operations all within a tourism experience. It is a novel concept of developing farms into vacation ventures with hospitality facilities helping the farms to generate additional revenue. Agri tourism can be defined as 'A range of activities, services and amenities provided by farmers and rural people to attract tourist to their area in order to generate extra income for their businesses'. Agri Tourism activities include farm tours, tractor and bullock cart rides, grapes, mangoes, and other horticulture farms and by-product farms; birds and animal farms, silk processing units and buildings like model Panchayat Ghars, community centers, water sheds etc. There are a lot of things the visitors or guests can enjoy in this agri tourism unit/farm. It is non massive tourism that is environmentally sustainable and adapted to local natural as well as social resources. In India this is a new concept but in most of the European countries the concept of Agri-Tourism had developed in the eighties. The farms that participate in agri tourism have doubled in countries like Italy, the United Kingdom, and France. In the middle of the nineties, 12 European countries (Belgium, Denmark, Greece, Netherlands, Portugal, Spain, Ireland, Great Britain, Italy, Austria, France and Germany) had more than 100.00 farm enterprises involved with different tourism activities. As per the study report of FICCI A.F. Ferguson and Co. 2004, every additional Rs. 10 lakhs invested can create 47.5 direct jobs and each direct job can create 11 indirect jobs. It also stated that every 30 million additional tourist translate into Rs. 4300 crores in revenue. It also stated that farm tourism if developed along unique indigenous lines could have a multiplier effect and high revenue capital ratio. A study by Agri Tourism Development Corporation reveals that within last 15 years, domestic tourism has grown by more than 304 million from 63 million in 1990 to 367 million in 2005 registering a growth of 20 per cent per annum.

Agri tourism is an innovative income generating strategy and activity for agri preneur. It is an instrument for employment generation, poverty alleviation and development. Agri tourism brings in together the declining agriculture sector and the booming tourism sector. The major primary sector agriculture gets closer to major service sector tourism and results in a win- win situation for both of them. While tourism sector has the potential to enlarge, the agriculture sector has the capacity to absorb expansion in tourism sector. The scope of agri-tourism is high because of the relative low cost of food, accommodation, recreation and travel. Agri-tourism, which involves villages and agriculture, has the capacity to satisfy the curiosity of the urban segment by providing scope for re-discovering the rural life, which is rich in diversity. It also provides family oriented recreational activities through rural games, festivals, food and dress. Peace and tranquility are in-built in Agri-tourism, so peoples usually find solace with nature friendly life style. For tourists it is like returning back to their roots. Agri-tourism also spreads knowledge about agriculture science where urban students are moving with the pace of technology. Agri-tourism also helps to reconcile farming interests and environmental protection through integrated land management in which farmers continue to play a key role. Tourists who choose farm accommodation rather than other kinds of accommodation facilities look for genuine rural atmosphere where they can share intimacy of the household they live in, learn traditional crafts and skills with their hosts, make friends which is a quality, modern times have almost forgotten and above all enjoy homemade food and drinks. It also serves as one of the greatest means of cultural exchange. The opportunities in the country are unlimited due to its varied climate, different agro-ecological zones, natural characteristics and socio-cultural entities. It can only be successfully initiated through the farmers' efforts. There are some guiding principles for Agri tourism to succeed. The tourists must have something to see like culture of the village, dress and festivals, something to do like participating in agricultural operations, riding camel, buffalo, cooking and participating in the rural games and finally something to buy like rural crafts, dress materials, fresh processed food etc. At the same it is the responsibility of the tourists not to disturb the nature.

9.16 Mobilizing Farmer Community

A community represents a microcosm of a nation. It can be effectively used to bring about changes that will benefit the social, emotional, financial and physical needs of its members. The tool to bring about changes is by mobilizing the farmer communities. Community mobilization is an attempt to bring both human and non-human resources together to undertake developmental activities in order to achieve sustainable development. It is a process through which action is stimulated by a community itself, or by others, that are planned, carried out, and evaluated by a community's individuals, groups, and organizations on a participatory and sustained basis to improve the overall standard of living in the community. The natural allies for mobilization are those persons who have a common interest in an issue. Participation is the key element for community mobilization. Today there is no dearth of good plans and programmes; but little progress has been made in translating ambitious plans into effective action. This is largely because the implementation is poor and the poor implementation is due to lack of peoples participation. Though we claim our commitment to participative approaches to helping the rural poor but our record of earlier community development and cooperatives efforts is largely a history of failure, resulting more often in strengthening the position of traditional elites than in integrating poorer elements into the national development process. Calls for involvement of the rural poor have come out little more than wishful thinking. The prevailing blueprint approach to development programming with its emphasis on detailed pre-planning and time bounded projects is itself cited as an important impediment. Mobilizing farmer communities through Self Help Groups, Farmer Interest Groups, Commodity Interest Groups is the need of the hour. These are unique in the sense that the members meet regularly, decide the plan of action and participate in the social and political sphere. The members support each other economically to meet consumptive and productive needs of the farmer members. A microfinance report released by NABARD said that as on March 2012, a total of 79.2 lakh SHG's with active bank linkages are operating in India. It has been able to ensure involvement of around 9.7 crore peoples with an aggregate bank balance of rupees 6,551 crores (Hazra, A 2012). What is encouraging is that the statistics indicate that over 90 per cent of SHG's in the country consist exclusively of women. The women SHG's have contributed immensely to their empowerment. These SHG members also motivate others to develop integrated natural resource based plans for better food security and livelihood opportunities. The small plans made by these SHG for small and marginal lands with locale specific cropping patterns can be integrated with other programmes through Gram Panchayats.These can a long way in enhancing the livelihood opportunities for rural poor and at the same time taking care of the already dwindling natural resources. The water use associations the producer associations, marketing cooperatives and the credit cooperatives are also an example of how the farmer communities mobilizes itself proactively for conserving the scarce natural resource and taking care of the credit and marketing needs of the farming community. The cooperatives are also one of the important means of empowering the farmers especially the women. In Haryana about 35,000 cooperative societies with a membership of about 46 lakh are in existence. Of the total, 700 cooperatives in the dairy sector exclusively for women have strength of about 39,000 members. About five milk plants and 27 milk chilling collection centers are working on a cooperative basis in the state (Lohumi, 2013). This ensures that the women members get a fair price of their milk.

These different forms of groups, associations and cooperatives all relate to community members and can network or are federated into farmer organizations at higher levels as has been the case of Maharashtra Grape growers association. Institutionalizing farmer participation must be an inbuilt component of the research. A community-based adaptive research capacity can only and only be achieved through work with groups of farmers rather than individuals and linking these up with research and extension agencies. Working with groups is a more decentralized process and less top-down than working with individuals. A group or collective action approach has proved to be an effective way of enhancing empowerment of farmers by increasing the bargaining power, getting the necessary forward as well as backward linkages and in influencing various policies not conducive to their occupation.

The cooperative model has already been established by Mr. Kurien, whose Gujarat Cooperative Milk Marketing Federation disburses rupees

15 crore in cash daily to its members. This milk cooperative model can be tries for food grains also. Marketing cooperatives also ensure fair remunerative prices to the farmers.

9.17 Cooperative Farming

Farms in India are characterized by not only being small but scattered also. The generational split of land has reduced the per capita availability of land in India to such an extent that the small fragmented piece of land have now become uneconomical. However, studies have also revealed that fragmentation is positively correlated to productivity due to more use of fertilizers and labour input. Another benefit associated with land fragmentation is the variety of soil and growing conditions that reduce the risk of total crop failure by giving the farmer a variety of soil and growing conditions. Raghbendra *et al.* (2005) investigated the impact of land fragmentation on technical efficiency of rice farms in India using the stochastic frontier method and confirmed that there was a significant positive relationship between farm size, average farm size and yield while the number of plots and yield were inversely related. Therefore fragmentation measured in terms of number of farms per household had a negative impact on yield.

Land fragmentation is defined as a multiplicity of non-contiguous plots within single ownership. A lot of time, money and resources get wasted in moving from one field to another. Small holdings also are an obstacle in agricultural mechanization. This has posed a serious challenge to the agricultural sector. It has been observed that as the size of farm increases the per hectare cost of different operations like ploughing, sowing harvesting decreases and scientific methods of cultivation, better irrigation and mechanization can be practiced with ease. Therefore the big question is how to place an effective alternative so that these fragmented holdings can be cultivated as a single compact unit. Consolidation of land holdings and Cooperative farming are two suitable options that have been in practice and can be replicated on a mass scale. Land consolidation means converting many small and fragmented land holdings into one. Farmers get one or two compact farms in lieu of their fragmented holdings. The whole process is done by firstly pooling all the fragmented holdings of the farmers and then reallocating them in such a way that each gets a suitable farm of having same total size and same fertility status like his previous fragmented holdings. Denmark in 1750 became the first country to start consolidation. India too had start consolidation of land holdings but the process has become a victim of benami transactions. In cooperative farming each farmer member remains the owner of his piece of land but do farming jointly. Profit is distributed among the member farmers on the basis of land owned and wages are distributed according to the number of days worked. The goal of Cooperative farming is to bring together all of the land resources of farmers in such an organized way that the farmers are collectively in a position to grow crops on every bit of land to the best of the fertility of the land. Several forms of Cooperative farming are in operation in different parts of the country. The 'Phad' in Kolhapur region and the 'Gallashi' in some parts of Andhra Pradesh are locally practiced ways of cooperative farming in the country. Land consolidation and Cooperative farming can also save the land wasted field boundaries. Also the surplus land can be used for creating community assets like schools, gardens and community halls.

9.18 The Orphan Crops

Modern agriculture generally focuses on the cultivation of three major staple crops (rice, maize and wheat) which provide about half the global human requirement for protein and calories. While about 7,000 plant species are found useful in agriculture, only about 150 species among them are largely used and less than 30 plant species meet about 90 per cent of world's food requirement. On the food front, currently about 60 per cent of calories and 50 per cent proteins are derived only from three major cereals, rice, wheat and maize (FAO, 1995). The emphasis on only a few of these belonging to cereal and other crop groups has left many other out of the priority. Such shrinking species content in the food basket is a matter of major concern (Frison *et al.*, 2006). This process has resulted in the marginalization of a large group of locally important crops. The contribution of these crops to nutrition security is largely unappreciated. These crops have been used for centuries or even millennia for their food, fibre, fodder, oil or medicinal properties, but have been reduced in importance over time. The reasons vary from poor consumer awareness to being unrecognized and being held in low esteem. What is worse is that with the modernization of agricultural practices some of them have been so neglected that genetic erosion of their gene pools has become so severe that they are often regarded as lost crops. Such crops have been called as Orphan/neglected or underutilized crops. There is some debate over the meaning of the terms orphan, neglected and underutilized crops. According to GFU for underutilized species, several criteria must be met for the crops to be considered as an orphan. These include proven food and energy value; the plant has been widely cultivated in the past or is cultivated on a limited geographical region.

The term orphan is usually used to describe crops that receive little scientific research or funding despite their significance for food security in the world's poorest regions (Naylor *et al.,* 2004). However the IPGRI for underutilized and neglected crops describes "Neglected crops are those grown primarily in their centers of origin or centers of diversity by traditional farmers, where they are still important for the subsistence of local communities. Some species may be globally distributed, but these tend to occupy special niches in the local ecology and in production and consumption systems". While these crops continue to be maintained by socio-cultural preferences and use practices, they remain inadequately characterized and neglected by research and conservation. They are i) locally plentiful but globally rare, ii) there is little scientific information and know ledge about them available and iii) their current use is limited, relative to their economic potential (Gruere *et al.* 2007).

The orphan crops are annually grown on more than 250 million hectares in developing countries. Their diversity lies from cereals like three minor millets, finger millet (*Eleusine coracana*), little millet (*Panicum sumatrense*) and foxtail millet (*Setaria itallica*) to legumes like Cowpea (*Vigna unguiculata*), root crops like Cassava (*Manihot esculenta*) and Pulse like rice bean (*Vigna umbellate*). All these are multipurpose but underutilized. India is no exception. These are crops which are vital for food security but whose potential have not yet been realized. These crops can be grown to address the food security of the resource poor farmers.

The fact is that these largely underutilized and neglected crops are vital for the national security of any country and more so in India where the National Food Security Act provides for the supply of coarse cereals to the target population. Their importance assumes more significance particularly because of their resilient characteristics to the harsh agro-climatic conditions, particularly in marginal soils, hilly terrain and under aberrant rainfall. These are well adapted to offer a dependable level of food security to the poor. and their better adoption to grow in marginal areas, with little or even no input conditions. They are also valued for their better nutritious profile of the grains and high quality straw. The extraordinary hardiness of many of these species and their ability to cope with adverse growing and climatic conditions offers great promise in the era of climate change (Bala Ravi *et al.*, 2006). There is an urgent need for mainstream research and development programs for these crops so that their potential value is not under-estimated and under-exploited any more. At the same time it is also necessary to create markets for them both at the national as well as global level so that the farmers can get better incentive of their produce and get motivated to produce more.

Table 29: Status of Orphan Crops in India

Crop	*Area (million hectare)*	*Production (million tonnes)*	*Productivity (kg/ha)*
Sorghum	7.38	7.0	949
Pearl millet	9.61	10.37	1079
Ground nut	5.86	8.26	1411
Pigeon pea	3.40	2.37	697
Chickpea	7.63	5.53	724

9.19 Agri-preneurship

While agri-preneurship as a concept is drawn from wider entrepreneurship and specific to agriculture. It is at present very critical and urgent. Agri-preneur is the one who plays the role of an entrepreneur in agriculture. The peculiarities of the country's agriculture sector such as inadequate technologies, weak extension linkages, low profitability and the dominance of marginal and small farmers, demands a dire need for agri-preneurship. Agriculture is the mainstay of Indian economy contributing about 14 per cent to the Gross Domestic Product (GDP). Agri-preneurship involves the socio-economic upliftment of the greater population through creation of new agri-business unit; agricultural commodities value chains and overall economic growth. Sudharani has defined agri preneurship as generally sustainable, community oriented, directly marketed agriculture (Uneze, C., 2013). The need for agri preneurship also originates from increasing demand for quality food products, health consciousness and changing consumption patterns and the need to reduce wastage and malnutrition. The aspects of agriculture that could be opened up for entrepreneurship include both the on-farm activities and off-farm ventures. The on-farm activities may involve production, processing, farm input manufacturing, and agro service ventures. Off-farm agri-preneurship ventures may include activity such as agri-tourism entrepreneurship.

Farmers are getting disillusioned with agriculture and going by the rate they are leaving agriculture it will not be wrong to say that the fortune of the agriculture sector in the country is dwindling. The 'culture' of agriculture needs to be replaced with 'preneur'. Given the present situation of the farming community in being helpless in making their ends meet, what is needed is to develop farmers as entrepreneurs who besides themselves can provide jobs to others also. Commodities can be turned into value added products and reasonable rates can be obtained from retail outlets across the country. A report of the committee of Planning commission on Angel investment and early stage venture capital (June 2012) states that India needs to create 10-15 million jobs per year for the next decade to provide gainful employment to its young population. Agriculture can be made to create huge opportunities in India. A country where most of the farmers are illiterate and are still baffling with conventional practices of crop production, they can earn huge profits by taking to entrepreneurship. There is a lot of scope in food processing, value addition, post harvest handling. With the same available resources, young entrepreneurs can create their own business models. BAIF in India has been actively engaged in promoting agri preneurship in livestock and Horticulture. Agri-clinics and Agribusiness Centers scheme is also catering to the needs of the unemployed youths in setting up their own ventures and emerging as successful agri-preneur. It has been discussed in detail in the previous chapter in the book. There are huge opportunities in agricultural entrepreneurship sector.

The practices of agriculture need to be transformed. Agri-entrepreneurship education has become increasingly necessary to be taught in the colleges, polytechnics and universities. This emphasis is because of the potential role of entrepreneurs in creating jobs and wealth and in fact promoting economic growth. The agri-preneur can demonstrate that given a fair chance they could play a part more effectively in transforming Indian agriculture to meet the emerging challenges of the sector.

Chapter 10
SUSTAINABLE AGRICULTURAL DEVELOPMENT

10.1 The Need for Sustainability

The non judicious use of our resources both natural as well as manmade has already caused enormous threat to land water and air. Although the green revolution led to increase in the production of our food grains; but this chemical intensive revolution threatened our basic existence in the biosphere. A constantly degrading environment has started to affect the crop yields across the world. The water table in states of Punjab, Haryana and Uttar Pradesh; the so called 'food bowls of the country has started receding. The water intensive cultivation in Punjab is causing ground water level to recede by 33 centimeters per day. The once fertile soil is now exhibiting signs of fatigue and severe nutrient deficiencies.

The most alarming development that followed the green revolution was the fast and massive replacement of other crops with cereals. In Punjab the available data indicates that between 1960-61 to 1999-2000 the net crop area under rice increased 10 times and that under wheat increased three times but during the same period the area under pulses declined by 10 folds so had the area under maize, oilseeds and millets. The massive use of non biodegradable pesticides during the green revolution has serious effects on health. It has led to the alarming increase in child miscarriage in pregnant mothers and contamination of mother's milk up to 400 per cent to 800 per cent above permissible limits. Such is the incidence of pollution that a weekly train runs from Bathindha in Punjab to Ganga Nagar in Rajasthan carrying farmers with cancer for cheaper treatments. The train is famous by the name of Cancer train. The use of Endosulfan in Kasaragod of Kerala state is another example of how the chemical intensive cultivation has been threatening the very existence of life on earth. In 2001, reports surfaced about the high incidence of cerebral palsy, women with strange gynecological disorders, learning disabilities, low intelligence quotient and scholastic backwardness among children of Padre village.

Another aspect of Green revolution was that major stress was laid on Paddy and Wheat and that too in irrigated conditions. The result was that there was an unprecedented apathy towards promoting dry land farming. As a result the enormous diversity of millets with proven nutrition values went into a declining phase (Ghosh, A., 2012). Reportedly till 1970 there were 10 to 15 insect pests of which five were considered as major pests. After the introduction of HYVs, at least 40 to 50 different invertebrates obtained pest status with 10 major pests. This obviously led to more expenditure being incurred for pest control and opened up the market for pesticide industry. The dependence of farmers on HYV seeds led to loss of more than 5000 folk rice varieties in West Bengal alone in the past 50 years. The farmer's varieties of seeds with such unique characters as ability to withstand salt in the soil have become rare. On April 15, 2008 something unusual happened. Some 401 scientists from 58 countries worked together under the aegis of World Bank, FAO, UNDP, WHO, UNICEF to come up with a report on agricultural knowledge, science and technology. The report is known all over the world as International Assessment of Agricultural knowledge, Science and Technology for Development (IAASTD). IAASTD has discussed virtually all issues directly or indirectly related to agriculture globally and regionally. The report marked the growth in world agricultural production but pointed out that the sharing of benefits has not been at all equitable and the enhanced production has been attained at a very high and social environmental cost. Global pesticide deaths are estimated at 22,000 annually with between 20 to 50 lakh peoples suffering from pesticide toxicity. The first green revolution made agriculture dependent on petroleum and chemical industry where as the second green revolution is mainly driven by biotech and seed firms. It is reported that over 100,000 different chemical compounds have entered the atmosphere and ecosystem as a bye product of manufacturing. The bee population also has seen a sharp decline due to indiscriminate use of pesticides and this may affect production of many fruit crops because bee is the most effective pollinator.

10.2 Sustainable Development

The term 'sustainable development' was coined by 'World commission on Environment and Development' headed by Gro Harlem Brundtland. The commission defined sustainable development as 'development that meets the need of present without compromising the ability of the future of generation to meet their own needs' (Brundtland, 1987). The US Congress arrived at an acceptable definition for sustainable agriculture (Stuart and Robinson, 1997) for the USDA and its Agricultural Research Service (ARS) after considerable national debate. By this definition, an agricultural production system is sustainable if, over the long term, it enhances or maintains the productivity and profitability of farming in the region, conserves or enhances the integrity and diversity of both the agricultural production system and the surrounding natural ecosystem, and also enhances health, safety, and aesthetic satisfaction of both consumers and producers.

Sustainability as a goal of agricultural research and development is a relatively recent concept. Now Indian Council of Agricultural Research (ICAR) has also revised its mandate; its new vision statement reads, "to harness science to ensure sustained physical, economic, and ecological access to food and livelihood security to all through generation, assessment, refinement, and adoption of appropriate technologies," (ICAR, 1999). All institutions of ICAR and State Agricultural Universities (SAUs), which constitute the NARS, have new vision statements focusing on "productivity with sustainability." For this major adjustments are needed in agricultural, environmental and macroeconomic policy, at both national and international levels, in developed as well as developing countries, to create the conditions for sustainable agriculture and rural development. Though a lot of progress has been made on the production front, disappointment is widely expressed at the slow progress in moving towards sustainable agriculture and rural development in many countries. Sustainable agriculture aims to increase food production and enhance food security in an environmentally sound way so as to contribute to sustainable natural resource management. Food security, although a policy priority for all countries-remains an unfulfilled goal. Agriculture helps to sustain rural life and land. We have all the potential to emerge as an agricultural power in the not too distant future if a better strategy is implemented. There is an urgent need to overhaul the social economic and farm policies to remove rural disparities and remove rural poverty. All these need to be addressed together. The face of rural India has to be transformed keeping in view the need to improve the living conditions of masses and diversification strategies have to be devised to bring more value addition while agricultural productivity has to be geared up. About two third of the country population still depends on agriculture and allied activities and lives in rural areas. There is an urgent need to ensure inclusive economic growth where benefits of economic growth are to percolate to the poor and underprivileged. It entails the enhancement of agricultural credit flow, revitalizing agricultural extension, training and research, providing employment to the needy and creating durable agriculture related assets and ensuring empowerment of the poor.

The focus of agricultural research has to be field oriented so as to ensure efficient use of resources and conservation of soil, water and ecology on substantive basis along with the introduction of new varieties of seeds modern technologies, nutrient and knowledge based intervention developed for different agro-climatic zones. Development is sustainable if it consumes resources no faster than they can be generated and a sustainable society is the one that satisfies its needs without diminishing the prospects of future generations (Desh Bandhu *et al.,* 1980). Even the US in its Farm Bill (1990) has defined sustainable system as, ' An integral system of plant and animal production that would over a long period satisfy human food fibre need, enhance environmental quality and natural resources based upon which agriculture economy depends.

10.3 Different Aspects of Sustainable Agriculture

10.3.1 Use of Integrated Techniques

Agriculture today has become a non remunerative enterprise. It is here pertinent to mention that that even in Punjab, where the average farm size is 3.8 acres which is 2.5 times the average size of Indian farms, the farmer's income is far less than the average salary of a class IV government employee. The NSSO survey also reveals that forty per cent of the respondents want to quit farming if other option was available to them. If we analyze the total cost of cultivation per hectare we, find that inputs and labour cost have a greater bearing on the farmers is income. The inputs especially the hybrid seeds which can be used only once, the chemicals in the form of fertilizers (though these are subsidized) and pesticides/weedicides/herbicides are not affordable to most of the farmers. The cost of these inputs and the labour costs can be minimized significantly if we use integrated techniques like integrated weed management, integrated pest management, integrated disease management and integrated nutrient management. This management techniques use a judicious mix of all the available methods to feed the plants and control the weeds, pests and diseases. One of the greatest advantages of these techniques is also that they are environmentally sound and ecologically safe. Also the use of local resources such as the Farm Yard Manure in INM, the use of bio agents in pest management and disease control largely reduce the dependence of farmers on chemicals. Presently agriculture sector provides employment to more than 50 per cent of the workforce, but most of this is disguised employment. With proper crop management practices the labour days can be minimized. These can contribute greatly in reducing the total cost of cultivation of the farming community ultimately making agriculture remunerative and a more economically viable option.

10.3.2 Sustainable Intensification

Sustainable intensification refers to the ways to increase agricultural production that are sustainable in the long run. It is to increase production while sustaining the natural resource base. Producing crops with crop intensification techniques have proved far better in terms of conserving resources, getting higher yields and more income for the farming communities. Small farmers around the world are dramatically boosting their productivity and yields by adopting System of Crop Intensification (SCI). These crop intensifications systems are characterized by simple modifications of agricultural practices that synergize to promote healthy plant growth. These modifications include improving soil conditions and greatly lowering plant density, without the use of synthetic pesticides or fertilizers. SCI methods are being adopted rapidly worldwide as they are low risk, do not require farmers to have access to unfamiliar technologies and save money on multiple inputs, while higher yields result in increased incomes. By system of Rice Intensification, a Paddy yield of 22.4 tons/ha reported by SRI trial plot of a farmer in Deveshpura Panchayat in Katri Sarai block of Nalanda district in Bihar is a world record surpassing the yield of 19 tons/hectare of China (Khan, 2012). The system increases yield, saves water, reduces production costs, and increases income.

10.3.4 Organic Farming

It is based on farm technologies that largely avoid or exclude the use of chemical fertilizers and pesticides and do not deteriorate the soil health. Organic farming is rather a movement that depends on the use of on farm and off farm crop residues, animal wastes and manures, green manure crops, crop rotations with leguminous crops. The basic philosophy behind the Organic farming is to feed the soil rather than the crop thereby giving back to nature what has been taken out from it. It is sort of farming with naturally occurring materials. It is regarded as a mean to bring about improvement in the production, quality improvements and to maintain the balance of nature. Some decrease in yield of crops in the initial years of organic farming has been reported but by feeding the soil by various nutrients it is considered sustainable one. Organic farming lays minimum reliance on artificial inputs such as fertilizers, pesticides, weedicides, growth regulators and other chemicals. Certification of the entire production and distribution chain up to the end products is an essential component of the Organic farming. Thus Organic farming is not product acclaimed but process acclaimed. Its adequate use improves the physical conditions of soil in terms of improvement holding capacity of the soil and improvement of the soil structure and soil aeration. The regular use improves the biological nature of the soil by enhancing the microorganism population and thereby improving the nutrient availability to the plants.

10.3.5 Using People's Wisdom: Indigenous Traditional Knowledge

The Brundtland Commission recognizes three type of agricultural systems (WCED, 1987). First, Industrial Agriculture, characterized by large farm units, high capitalization, high input-independent and often at times, subsidies-supported; second, Green Revolution Agriculture, characterized by a mixture of small and large farms which exploit high-yielding varieties with complementary inputs; and third, Low Resource or Resource-Poor Agriculture, characterized by small farm units, fragile soils, rain dependency and minimum inputs. Agriculture in India is characterized by the presence of marginal and small land holdings which are fast losing their fertility due to indiscriminate use of chemical fertilizers. With about sixty per cent of the total cultivated area in rainfed zone, agriculture in India is rightly called the 'gamble of monsoons'. The Green Revolution technologies, which partly solved the problem of food and fibre needs, appeared to be too expensive, as the costs of technology transfer, soil erosion and loss of plant genetic materials that were resistant to diseases are high. At last we have realized the hazardous effects of the chemical intensive agriculture. Today the scientific community all over the Globe is thinking of alternatives to this conventional approach. Article 8(j) of the Convention of Biological Diversity (Rio, 1992) has also contributed to this process by requiring signatories to, "respect, preserve and maintain knowledge, innovations and practices of indigenous and local communities embodying traditional life-styles relevant for the conservation and sustainable use of biological diversity".

Many of the problems we face today can be solved with our Indigenous Technical Knowledge (ITK). It is an integral part of the culture and history of a local community. Indigenous technologies can serve as alternative to these problems since they are practiced from time immemorial, perfected by the trial and error over generations and standardized (Chambers, 1989). These have evolved through many years of regular experimentation on the day to day life and available resources surrounded by the community and are developed around specific condition of men and women indigenous to a particular geographical area. ITK is unwritten body of knowledge. It is held in different brains.

It is a dynamic system, ever charming, adopting and adjusting to the local situations and has close links with the culture, civilization and religious practices of the communities (Pushpangadan *et al.*, 2002).

Haverkort (1995) defined Indigenous Traditional Knowledge is the actual knowledge of a given population that reflects the experiences based on tradition and includes more recent experiences with modern technologies.

ITK is dynamic and it changes through creativity and innovativeness as well as through contact with other local and international knowledge systems (Warren, 1991). These knowledge systems represent mechanisms to ensure minimal livelihoods for local people. In our daily life, we often come across various ITK related practices. Farmers use Kerosene oil soaked chord to keep away the case worm (*Nymphela depunctalis*) in rice. About 70 to 80 per cent of the worms are controlled by this method. Farmers keep the effigy of a man like toy made of rice straw wearing white dress in the center of field at time of milking to grain filling stage to reduce the bird menace in almost all parts of the country. Farmers in Jammu and Kashmir and North India usually treat Paddy seeds with cow dung for a night prior to broadcasting. This increases the germination percentage of the seeds.

Bhang (*Cannabis sativa*) plant are uprooted and kept in standing water in Paddy fields to kill the thread worms. If, the problem is severe then crushed leaves are put in the standing water to kill the thread worms is applied. In Uttar Pradesh in certain areas Kerosene Oil @ 2.5 litres per acre in termite affected Paddy at the time of irrigation to repel termites. Leaf twigs, bark and seeds of Azadirachta Indica and Rhizomes of Acorus Calamus are used to control insect pests of stored grains. Leaves and stem of Nicotiana Glauca are used to control Ear head bug and leaf feeders. Leaves and Twigs of Calotropis Procera are used to control Pests of cucurbits. These practices are also used in many parts of the country Application of Lime @ 30kg/acre and oil cake @ 45 kg/acre can manage the problem of soil salinity. Incorporating Diancha before Paddy Cultivation also reduces the effect of salinity in paddy crop.

(Mathuraman and Meera, 2010)

Peoples have also used their traditional wisdom for validation of IPM techniques. *Cacia fistula* (locally known as Karongal) saves Mustard crop from aphid attack. Both the plants have yellow flowers and aphid is attracted towards yellow colour. *Cacia fistula* plantation on the bunds with profuse flowering diverts the attack of aphids to itself instead of mustard crop thereby saving the precious crop. Such a practice after getting scientific validation is known as one of IPM techniques.

At the grassroots level it is, obviously most important for the local community in which the bearers of such knowledge live and produce. What is needed today is to critically validate the ITK against the usefulness for their intended objectives. Indigenous knowledge forms part of the global knowledge. In this context, it has a value and relevance in itself. It needs to be documented. The developmental strategy cannot override indigenous traditional knowledge. Today the use of chemicals like fertilizers and pesticides have already inflicted irreversible damage to our ecosystem and rising cost of inputs have made the farming non remunerative. The use of ITK for soil health improvement, crop production, conserving resources and also in livestock management can go a long way in reducing the cost of cultivation, and increase the yields with little threat to our planet ultimately leading to sustainability in different farming systems.

10.4 Paid Ecological Services

The Millennium Ecosystem Assessment, a 2005 UN-sponsored report designed to assess the state of the world's ecosystems assessed twenty four specific ecosystem services and reported that the unsustainable land use has caused irreversible loss of biodiversity affecting 15 of the 24 ecosystem services that were examined. The human interference with nature has resulted in soil degradation, air and water purification, climate regulation, natural hazards and pest outbreaks. It was thought of providing some incentives to the peoples who will make some efforts towards promoting conservation of natural resources. Payments for ecosystem services (PES) emerged in response to this. Payments for environmental services are incentives offered to farmers or landowners in exchange for managing their land to provide some sort of ecological service. These are a transparent system for the additional provision of environmental services through conditional payments to those who provide it voluntarily with the ultimate aim of conservation of natural resources. Payments for Ecosystem Services (PES) value ecosystem services conservation and increase income generation in rural areas, food security and sustainable development. PES schemes can be found in all continents. Most PES schemes revolve around three groups of ecosystem services: water and soil-related services, climate stabilization, and biodiversity conservation. We often overlook the social benefits accruing from the conservation efforts and only monetary benefits are taken into consideration. The PES concept has now been expanded to also include social benefits arising from agricultural production activities. The social benefits include the rural employment generation, reduction of rural migration, creation of community assets and community cohesion are some of the social aspects that do not find a mention.

Payment for ecosystem services for agriculture is an economic instrument designed to provide incentives to increase positive externalities from agriculture, meet the conservation costs and benefit the society as a whole. Regarding markets for PES, it can be developed by making consumers aware of the importance of food produced in a fresh and healthy environment. FAO also analyzed 286 local PES and PES like schemes from 57 countries and found that the concept of PES for agricultural sustainability was spreading (Mann, S. K. 2014). Major PES transactions in the world have been associated with land use changes like reforestation and watershed protection. In India the concept is now but has been practiced in many countries for quiet some years. A national PES programme was initiated in Costarica in 1996 when the term was used for first time by changing the forest law and creating a legal framework to pay land owners for provision of ecosystem services. In Nicaragua, Costa Rica, and Columbia an integrated PES projects for silvi pastoral practices is also being implemented in a few thousand hectares.

In Kullu's Great Himalayan National Park, the communities patrolling the area are paid rupees 5,000 annually by the government if no fires occur in the area they patrol. The Forest Conservation Law in the country also mandates that the projects converting forestlands make payments to the users which are deposited in a centrally managed fund with CAMPA. India also faces the heat due to the unsustainable practices, it needs to devise and formulate policies right from the national to micro level to promote various PES for sustainable agriculture. This will result in rejuvenating degraded agri-ecosystem and environmental services.

10.5 Family Farms

Ensuring food security for millions of peoples all over the globe is an urgent priority. The green revolution, no doubt helped us to increase food production but it proved unsustainable in the long run. The need therefore has aroused to find out more sustainable ways that do not compromise with the future generations. Family farming has now been recognized as a key to ensuring food security for all. Such is the focus on Family farming that the United Nations has declared 2014 the 'International Year of Family Farming' to highlight the role that family farmers play. The family farmers include small and medium sized farmers, the traditional communities many of which are rich in indigenous technical knowledge, the pastoralists, the forest dwellers, food gatherers and all those that have a role to play in food security and sustainable development.

There are more than 570 million farms in the world. More than 90 percent of farms are run by an individual or a family and rely primarily on family labour. The United Nations also released a report in this International Year of Family Farming, 'The State of Food and Agriculture 2014: Innovation in family farming (SOFA 2014).' According to the report as per the number of family farms, families run about nine out of ten farms. The report also came out with the finding that family farms occupy a large share of the world's agricultural land and produce about 80 percent of the world's food. These farms representing the dominant form of agriculture in most countries range in size from tiny, subsistence holdings to large-scale, commercial enterprises, producing a vast range of food and cash crops in all kinds of agro-ecological conditions. The definition of family farm vary but the International Steering Committee for the International Year of Family Farming (2014) has given the following conceptual definition of family farming as, 'Family Farming (which includes all family-based agricultural activities) is a means of organizing agricultural, forestry, fisheries, pastoral and aquaculture production which is managed and operated by a family and predominantly reliant on family labour, including both women's and men's. The family and the farm are linked, co-evolve and combine economic, environmental, social and cultural functions. In a survey that comprised of about 36 definitions of family farm, every definition specified that the farm is owned, operated and/or managed at least partly by a member of the household; many specify a minimum share of labour contributed by the owner and his/her family; many set upper limits on the land area or sales of the farm; and some also set upper limits on the share of household income derived from non-farm activities (Garner and de la O Campos, 2014). A family farm requires that the farm be partially or entirely owned, operated and/or managed by an individual and her/his relatives.

The vast majority of the world's farms are small or very small, and in many low-income countries farm sizes are becoming even smaller. This has also become a compulsion due to the generational split of land. Worldwide, it has been reported that farms of less than 1 hectare account for 72 percent of all farms and these control only 8 percent of all agricultural land; larger farms between 1 and 2 hectares account for 12 percent of all farms and these control 4 percent of the land, while farms in the range of 2 to 5 hectares account for 10 percent of all farms and these control 7 percent of the land. Contrary to this only 1 percent of all farms in the world are larger than fifty hectares, but see the difference; these few farms control 65 percent of the world's agricultural land. It has been reported that small and medium-sized farms tend to have higher agricultural crop yields per hectare than larger farms. It is because these small and medium sized farms manage their resources well and use labour more intensively. A large proportion of family farmers with small landholdings also depend on other natural resources. Those living on the peripheries of forests depend largely on forest produces, and those residing in coastal areas rely heavily on fisheries and other aquatic produce. One can thus acknowledge that the share of small and medium sized farms in national food production is likely to be even larger than the share of land they manage. Today there is a wide spread acknowledgement that we need another revolution but that responds to today's needs and looks to the future. When the United Nations is celebrating this year as the International day of Family Farming; it itself speaks volumes of the world wide recognition given to the family farms.

However, the intensive resource use on these farms may threaten sustainability of production. It has been seen that while smaller farms tend to achieve higher yields per hectare, their output per worker. Agriculture therefore is considered a case of disguised employment. As increased labour productivity is a necessary precondition for sustained income growth we have to enable families in these low income countries to rise their per worker output. In India too, there exists a large gap between the actual yields that are obtained from fields and the potential yields that can be obtained from them. These large gaps between actual and potential yields for major crops in India can be significantly reduced through productivity growth on family farms. What is needed is to develop new technologies and remove various bottlenecks that hinder the adaptation of existing as well as new technologies. The past practice of chemical input led cultivation cannot meet our goal of sustainable agriculture production. Productivity growth has to be obtained along with the conservation of our natural resources. At the same time we have to improve their livelihoods by providing them necessary inputs at the right time, building their resilience particularly towards climate change, providing them the necessary linkages with the markets. The family farms are very much a part and parcel of our endaveour to achieve food security and sustainable development that minimizes the risk of environmental degradation and also loss to our bio diversity. It would not be wrong to say that food security of the poor and food insecure also depends on these diverse 570 million family farms. Our innovation and extension strategies must consider their agro-ecological and socio-economic conditions and see that the agricultural research and development, the mobilization strategy, the advisory services, the markets does not bye pass this group.

10.6 Protecting Farmers' Rights: PPV and FRA

Farmers of the country have developed technologies which are unique in the area and are locale specific. They have come up with plant varieties which they have developed after careful selection of the plants for so many generations. But, what is disgusting is that the farmers intellect is not being properly recognized and their wisdom seldom finds a place in the policy making process. Even the various farmer bodies across the countries are serving the purpose of solving political unemployment. They are being headed by political leaders.

Let us take the case of seeds. The farmers have developed so many indigenous seed varieties of different crops that in the absence of an adequate legislation the Indian markets would have been flooded by seed of foreign companies and ultimately we would have lost to these foreign companies. The result would have been that most of the indigenous varieties of seeds had become a thing of the past. As India is a signatory to the WTO proposals, and also had ratified the Trade Related Aspects of Intellectual Property rights agreement, it has to opt for protecting the rights of farmers and plant breeders. This was also necessary to ensure that the farmer's rights are not being eroded. As such, the country thus came up with a legislation; The Protection of Plant Varieties and Farmers Rights Act (PPV and FRA) that gives farmer legal claim over the seeds developed by them. The Act also has some similarities with the International Union for the Protection of New Varieties of Plants (UPOV, 1978) but some additional provisions have been incorporated in the act to safeguard the interests of the breeding institutions as well as the farmers. The legislation acknowledges the farmer as a cultivator, conserver and producer of seed. The act provides for the establishment for an effective system for protection of plant varieties, the rights of farmers and the plant breeders besides encouraging development of new plant varieties.

The (PPV and FRA) was enacted on October 30, 2001; the rules notified on September 12, 2013 and The Protection of Plant Varieties and Farmers Rights Authority established by the Government of India on November 11, 2006. The authority operates under the Ministry of Agriculture and Cooperation, Government of India and is headed by the Chairperson who enjoys authority equivalent to the Secretary to the Government of India. The Chairman is appointed by the government of India and has 15 more members. Of the fifteen eight are ex-officio representing various departments and ministries of Government of India, three are from State Agricultural Universities and the state governments, one representative each from farmers, tribal organizations, seed industry and women organization that is associated with agricultural activities. The functions of the PPV and FR authority include registration of new plant varieties and to ensure availability of seeds of the registered varieties under the provisions of compulsorily licensing. The section 39 of the Act that covers Farmers rights include farmers who bred or develop a new variety. Farmers' variety refers to a variety that has been traditionally cultivated and evolved by farmers in their fields or as a wild relative or a land race of a variety about which the farmers possess the common knowledge. Under

Section 45 of the Gene Fund of PPV and FR Act, the farmers who also contribute in conservation of plant genetic resources, the wild relatives and their improvement through selection and preservation are also entitled for recognition and award. Any farmer who bred or develops a new variety is entitled for registration in the same manner as a plant breeder. The farmers' can register that variety which they had bred or developed and also have the authority to sow, use, exchange, resow or sell his farm produce including seed of a registered variety. They are also are exempted from any kind of fee in respect of any proceedings, inspection of any document or obtaining any court decision. But for registration of plant varieties farmers have to pay the prescribed fee.

The act also compensates for the crop failure. The section 39(2) of the act, says that in case a registered varieties failed to germinate well in the given conditions, the farmers be suitably compensated by the company from which he had purchased seed. Besides the rights of farmers, the rights of the breeders, the researchers and the community rights are also taken care of in the act. In 2008, a National Register of Plant Varieties was opened which contains the name of all the registered plant varieties with the names and addresses of their respective breeders and their rights in respect of the registered varieties. The authority has also established a National Gene Bank and National Gene Fund. The National Gene Bank stores the seed material including parental lines submitted by the breeder of the registered variety.

10.7 Futures Market

Farmers in India face not only yield risk but price risk as well. This traditional system does not fetch them remunerative prices for their produce The private guilds of middlemen, commission agents at the sabzi mandis, street vendors and vegetable sellers in the retail market work in tandem to make huge profits on sale of commodities sold by farmers. In case of perishable commodities, the farmer cannot wait for a better price. These guilds exploit both the farmer and the consumer as the farmers' share in the consumer price keeps falling even as the consumer keeps paying more. Futures market has emerged as an alternative in forecasting the future prices of the commodities thus enabling the farming community to fetch more income by eliminating the scope of middlemen and plan their cropping pattern accordingly. A futures market is an auction market in which participants buy and sell commodity/future contracts for delivery on a specified future date. The number of commodity markets in the pre-independence era was limited, and there were no uniform guidelines or regulations: trade depended on mutual trust and social control. In India, agriculture has traditionally been an area with heavy government intervention. Government intervenes by trying to maintain buffer stocks, they try to fix prices, have import-export restrictions and a host of other interventions. In this case, the question arises about who will maintain the buffer stock, how will we smoothen the price fluctuations, how will farmers not be vulnerable that tomorrow the price will crash when the crop comes out, how will farmers get signals that in the future there will be a great need for wheat or rice. In all these aspects the futures market has a very big role to play. If it is presumed that there will be a shortage of wheat tomorrow, the futures prices will go up today, and it will carry signals back to the farmer making sowing decisions today. In this fashion, a system of futures markets will improve cropping patterns. If the farmer is growing wheat and is worried that by the time the harvest comes out prices will go down, then he can sell the wheat in the futures market at a price which is fixed today, which eliminates risk from price fluctuations. Thus the farmer would like to lock in his future price and not be exposed to fluctuations in prices. The National Multi Commodity Exchange (NMCE) was the first exchange to be granted permanent recognition by the government, where futures trading commenced on 26 November, 2002 in 24 commodities. The Multi Commodity Exchange of India (MCX) was established in November 2003 and the National Commodity and Derivatives Exchange Limited (NCDEX) commenced operations in December 2003. Today, futures trading are permissible in 95 commodities in India. There are 25 recognized futures exchanges with more than 3000 registered members. Trading platforms can be accessed through 20,000 terminals spread over 800 towns/cities. The volume of trade in the exchanges in 2006-07 was Rs.36.77 lakh crore, 97.2 per cent of which is accounted for by the four national exchanges, *viz.* National Commodity and Derivatives Exchange Ltd. (NCDEX), Bombay; Multi Commodity Exchange (MCX), Bombay; National Multi Commodity Exchange (NMCE), Ahmadabad; and National Board of Trade (NBOT), Indore. The commodity exchanges are regulated by the Forward Markets Commission (FMC), which was established in 1952. In terms of value of trade, agricultural commodities constituted the largest commodity group in the futures market till 2005-06 (55.32 per cent). Since 2006-07, bullion and metals has taken this place. Between April 2007 and January 2008, agriculture futures amounted to Rs.7.34 lakh crore, 23.22 per cent of all commodity futures.

But, whether or not futures trading contributed to the increase in prices was a hotly debated subject. Some claimed that futures markets benefit the farmers and don't contribute to price rises, while others argued that speculation had led to price distortion. The Abhijit Sen Committee, constituted to examine the subject, only said that a cause and effect relationship between future and spot prices can't be established conclusively. Many agriculture economists understand the need of futures markets as an instrument for making Indian agriculture highly remunerative enterprise. The exchange-specific problems like thin volume and low market depth, infrequent trading, lack of effective participation of trading members, non-awareness of futures market among farmers, poor physical delivery, absence of a well-developed grading and standardization system and market imperfections have been found as the major deficiencies retarding the growth of futures market. The future of futures market, in respect of agricultural commodities in India calls for a more focused and pragmatic approach from the government.

Chapter 11
OUT OF BOX SOLUTIONS

A strong agriculture sector is very necessary for food and nutritional security of the country. No doubt, we have attained the record food grain production of more than 250 million tonnes, but at the same time we cannot be complacent given the increasing population and the increasing percentage of those leaving the farm sector. Given the woes the agriculture sector is facing today it needs to be looked at differently, unconventionally and with a new perspective. This chapter is devoted to some of these mentioned as under:

11.1 Interlinking of Rivers

It was about two centuries ago that Sir Arthur Cotton conceived the idea of interlinking of rivers. The ministry of water resources, government of India way back in 1980 formulated a National Perspective Plan (NPP) for development of water resources. The plan envisaged the inter basin transfer of water from surplus basins to water deficit basins. A National Water Development Agency (NWDA) was set up to carry out technical studies to establish the feasibility of NPP. NWDA identified 30 links 16 under peninsular component and 14 under Himalayan component for preparation of feasibility report. The link proposal firmed up by NWDA under NPP envisage additional irrigation benefit of 25 million hectare of irrigation from surface water, 10 million hectare by increased use of ground water and generation of 34,000 MW of power apart from the benefits of flood moderation, navigation, water supply, fisheries, salinity, pollution control etc. However the project is still pending and outcome is subjected to the consensus among the states involved in the project. Economic investigations have also revealed that with the adoption of micro irrigation system with an investment of rupees 12,50,000 crores and interlinking the rivers with an additional investment of rupees 7,50,000 crores to harvest the flood waters draining into the sea an area of 175 million hectares in the country can be brought under irrigated agriculture (Mahalingam, N. 2012). Besides this 30 million hectares can be brought under sugarcane cultivation to generate 4500 million tonnes of sugarcane which then can be converted to 25 million tonnes of sugar, 5 million tonnes of Jaggery, 300 billion litres of ethanol for fuel and 350 billion kwh of power that will help to generate produce valued at rupees 35,00,000 crores.

11.2 Nanotechnology

A Japanese Engineer Norio Taniguchi is credited with coining the word Nano Technology and Dr. Kim Erec Drexler an American Engineer is credited with popularizing the potential of nanotechnology. In simple words it is the creation of new products with different physical properties by manipulation of individual atoms and molecule. The definition of nanotechnology is based on the prefix "nano" which is from the Greek word meaning "dwarf". In more technical terms, the word "nano" means size of one billionth of something and is generally used when referring to materials with the size of 0.1 to 100 nanometres.

11.2.1 Nanotechnology in Agriculture

Agriculture in the developing countries is beset with many issues. These countries are facing the problem of malnutrition, low farm yields, land degradation, rising temperatures and the non profitable farming due to high cost of inputs. Nanotechnology thus has the potential to revolutionize agriculture. Nanofertilizers are more efficient than conventional fertilizers. These prevent build up of the nutrients in the soil thereby eliminating the risk of eutrophication and drinking water contamination. Take the case of the first nano-organic-iron chelated fertilizer in the world produced in Iran. It is reported to have unique features like ultra high absorption, increases production from 20 to 200 per cent, results in a rise of Photosynthetic rate by 3.5 times and a 70 per cent expansion in the leaves. Lithovit is also a naturally occurring CO_2 foliar spray made from Limestone deposits. It enhances the plant growth and results in high productivity by means of increasing the natural photosynthesis on supplying carbon dioxide (CO_2) at optimum concentration, which is much higher than that in the atmosphere and at the same time does not results in an increase of the CO_2 in the atmosphere which might create a climatic problem particularly when threat of Global warming looms large over agriculture. Similarly a plant growth regulator Nano-Gro is also based on Nanotechnology. The active ingredients in Nano-Gro came as package in coded sugar pellets less than [1" in diameter. These pellets are dissolved in ordinary water to create a powerful working solution. Just one pellet is capable of treating 42 kg of wheat seeds or 33 tomato plants. At this rate, one kilo of Nano-Gro can be used on enough seeds to plant 3,333 hectares of wheat or almost 700,000 tomato plants. Nano-Gro is a plant growth regulator and immunity enhancer. Employing chemical concentrations in the order of one part per billion, Nano-Gro stands apart from any product in the market. Different from fertilizers, Nano-Gro is not a source of nutrients for the plants. Nano-Gro does not contain hormones and does not, in any way changes the genetic structure of a plant.

Nano-Gro helps the plant naturally experience improved growth and enhanced health benefits resulting from the proper application of the principles of Agro Nanotechnology. Results show an increase of about 10 per cent in both protein and sugar content of treated plant for most types of crops.

The major role for nanotechnology-enabled devices is the use of autonomous nano sensors linked into the GPS system. The nano sensors can be distributed throughout the field where they can monitor soil conditions and crop. USA and Australia have already exploited this technology. Certain vineyards in California have installed WiFi technology with the help of the IT Company, Accenture. Although the initial cost of installing such a system is high but it is justified by the fact that it enables the best grapes to be grown which in turn produce finer wines, which command a premium price. The use of such wireless networks is of course not restricted to vineyards. Small nano sensors are being used by

Honeywell (a R and D company) to monitor grocery stores in Minnesota. This technology enables shop keepers to identify food items which have passed their expiry date and also reminds them to issue a new purchase order. The global market for wireless sensors is expected to reach be 7 billion USD by 2010.11. Ultimately, precision farming, with the help of smart sensors, will allow enhanced productivity in agriculture by providing accurate information, thus helping farmers to make better decisions.

11.2.5 Nanofood

Nanofood refers to the food made with use of Nanotechnological tools during cultivation, production, processing, or packaging of the food materials. Nanotechnology is a boon for the Food processing industry. The scope of Nanotechnology in food processing involves smart packaging, on demand preservatives, and interactive foods. Nano capsules containing flavour or colour enhancers, or added nutritional elements would remain dormant in the food and only be released when triggered by the consumer. The nutritional quality of food through can also be enhanced through selected additives and improving the way the body digests and absorbs food.

11.2.6 Strong Precise Delivery Systems

All over the world the agricultural production increased with increased use of chemical fertilizers and pesticides but it also brought with it the ill effects of the pesticides and chemicals in terms of disturbance of the ecological food chains and the land degradation. Many of the pesticides, including DDT were later found to be highly toxic, affecting human and animal health and as a result the entire ecosystem. Some of them such as Endosulfan have now been banned. Nanoscale devices are now used in agriculture. These devices are used to identify plant health before these become visible to the farmer. These devices will alert the farmer for timely remedial action. Such devices could also be used to deliver chemicals in a controlled and targeted manner. Nanomedicines are now used to treat different diseases such as cancer in animals with high precision, and targeted delivery to specific tissues and organs. Encapsulation and controlled release of pesticides have revolutionized the use of pesticides and herbicides. Now many formulations are available which contain nanoparticles within the range of 100-250 nm. These are able to dissolve in water more effectively than existing ones thus increasing their activity. Nanoemulsions *i.e.* emulsions of nano scale particles which can be either water or oil-based containing uniform suspensions of pesticidal or herbicidal nanoparticles of the size of 200-400 nm can be easily incorporated in various media such as gels, creams, liquids etc, and have multiple applications for preventative measures, treatment or preservation of the harvested product. Syngenta is using Nanoemulsions in its pesticide products. One of its successful growth regulating products.is the Primo MAXX plant growth regulator, which if applied prior to the onset of stress such as heat, drought, disease or traffic can strengthen the physical structure of turf grass, and allow it to withstand ongoing stresses throughout the growing season. Karate ZEON is another quick release product containing the active compound lambda-cyhalothrin and having a broad control spectrum on primary and secondary insect pests of cotton, rice, peanuts and soybeans.

11.2.7 Food Packaging and Processing

Nano particles are used to prolong the shelf life of many products by developing smart packages. Such packages are able to repair small holes, tears and respond to environmental changes of temperature, humidity and moisture. These packs alert the customer if the food is contaminated. Companies have developed Nano sensors which are extremely sensitive to gases released by food as it spoils, causing the sensor strip to change colour as a result, giving a clear visible signal of whether the food is fresh or not. EU researchers have developed biochips which detect pathogens in the meat and fish products. Now Nano capsules have been developed that are incorporated into food to deliver nutrients and for increased absorption of nutrients. Nano capsules containing tuna fish oil which is a source of omega 3 fatty acids are incorporated in bread in Australia. These are designed to break open only when they have reached the stomach, thus avoiding the unpleasant taste of the fish oil.

Whatever be the impact of nanotechnology on agriculture the safety of food will remain the prime concern. Application of Nano technological tools to agriculture is at its nascent stage, and its success will be based on its ultimate acceptance by the stakeholders. At the same time an effective regulatory mechanism and strong governance system made with involvement of all stakeholders should be put in place. Equal importance needs to be given to the societal issues associated with nanotechnology otherwise it will turn out to be another Genetically Modified Organisms (GMO) like controversy.

11.3 Using Renewable Energy Sources

Renewable energy sources such as solar power, wind power and biomass have potential to be utilized as supplementary energy source. As biomass and animal power are available locally these can meet the major energy needs of the rural sector. It is estimated that more than 600 million tonnes of biomass is available from various crop residues and agro-wastes of which about 60 –65 per cent can be used for power generation. Besides about 27 million tonnes municipal waste is also available which has potential to be utilized for energy production.

11.3.1 Using Solar Power and Wind Power in Agriculture

One thousand units (1000 kWh) of coal based electricity generation emit 900 kg carbon dioxide and if diesel is used for the same amount of electricity generation, it emits 300 kilogram carbon dioxide. Erratic supply of conventional sources of energy, escalating fuel prices and concern for the environment and sustainable development has provided renewable thrust to the development and dissemination of renewable energy driven practices. The clean development mechanisim also demands every country which is a signatory to it to comply with emission limitations. Each carbon credit or certified emission reduction (CER) is equivalent to the reduction of one ton of Carbon dioxide equivalent. Electricity is a major source of energy for all the agricultural operations in India. Government of India spends about 6 crores (60 million) rupees for installing 1 MW capacity of electricity generation. This is equivalent to rupees 60,000/- per KW or roughly 1100 Euro per KW. The electricity generation in India besides being too costly also is environmentally not safe. Also the huge amount of subsidy the government has to provide to the farmers leads to financial deterioration of the country's fiscal health. As such other alternatives need to be tried. Of different renewable resources of energy, the ones that India is best endowed with are wind and solar.

11.3.1.1 Solar Energy

Solar energy is more readily available than wind or other forms of renewable energy. India, sitting aside the Tropic of Cancer is blessed with abundant sunlight. The IWEA estimates that India has an onshore potential of at least 65 Giga watts or half the current total energy requirement of the country. But the current installed capacity is over 7 GW, making India the fourth largest producer of wind energy in the world. This indicates vast growth possibilities for the industry. One thousand solar pumps rating 3 Kilowatt each and at 19 per cent plant load factor will generate around 4500 carbon credits. Rajasthan has one of the best solar insolation on earth (6-7KWH/m^2/day) combined with 320 sunny days in a year. About 4000 farmers in Rajasthan have been benefitted using this scheme of being provided with solar energy tapping technology. With the mandatory drip irrigation, 48 million cubic meters of water has been saved and 2.4 million litres of diesel. The annual savings in foreign exchange is rupees 48 million. An assessment of the solar pump scheme by Mumbai IIT's Rakesh Dalal in June 2013 year showed that 50 per cent of the farmers were able to recover their investments within a year or two. Though Punjab also has been using solar pumps for quite some time, but the success has not been as that of Rajasthan which has integrated use of water and energy through modern technology. Efficient pumping of water through solar energy is innovatively linked to water harvesting and drip irrigation. With every 1000 solar water pumps used there is an annual saving of six lakh litres of conventional diesel fuel reducing carbon foot prints (Usha Rai).

11.3.1.2 Wind Power in Agriculture

Using wind power in agriculture is the most feasible option to check all the negativities associated with electricity generation. The advantage is that it is a perennial source and available day and night. It is also the most useful energy source for those low lying isolated, hilly and coastal regions. Germany has taken the lead in producing wind power. India ranks fourth as for as production of wind power is concerned. According to a study by the CSTEP, wind energy is cost-effective as compared with other sources of generation. Government of India has estimated the potential of 45000 MW of wind power throughout the country. So far about 3500 MW capacity has been installed in India. All this power is obtained through big wind turbines from 250 KW to 1250 KW capacity. In fact, there is a huge potentiality of small wind turbines in India. As per estimates, roughly 100000 MW power can be produced in India from only small wind turbines up to 10 KW. There are bright prospects to establish about 50 million small wind turbines from 500W to 10KW capacity.

In India the agriculture is characterized by and marginal and small farms. There are about 100 million small farmers in India. So there is a possibility of small wind turbine in every farm and every small factory where ever there is a wind. So millions of small wind turbines can be installed in small farms of India making farmers self reliant in electricity for their own use, for water pumping and other agricultural processing small industries. If small wind turbines are promoted in India, every farmer can supply excess power to the grid and thus power shortage can be avoided. One disadvantage of wind is that its generation is not viable in all parts. The second is that virtually nowhere in the world is wind power usable at all times. There are times when there is no wind or it is blowing too slow or too fast to be used.

11.4 Using Space for Agriculture

The important applications where space can be used for the benefit of agriculture are precision farming, remote sensing, weather forecasting, disaster management, irrigation potential assessment, command area development, water shed development, agricultural drought assessment etc. Use of meteorological satellites and radars allow very accurate prediction of rainfall. The different hydrological models can provide early warning and risk of flooding as well as soil moisture build up.

11.4.1 Precision Farming

Precision farming provides a new solution using a systems approach for today's agricultural issues such as the need to balance productivity with environmental concerns. It is based on advanced information technologies. It includes describing and modeling variations in soils and plant species and integrating agricultural practices to meet site specific requirements. It aims at increased economic returns, as well as at reducing the energy input and the environmental impact of agriculture. Application of right quantity of inputs at the right time and at right place is one of the prerequisite for successful crop production. Unfortunately, most of our farmers do not have any idea about the right time and right placement of chemicals. Their broadcasting methods seldom take into account the inter and intra field variability. Precision farming enables us to have the right amount of inputs in the right place and at the right time which benefits crops, soils, groundwater, and thus the entire crop cycle.

Precision farming (PF) also called satellite farming or site specific crop management (SSCM) is a farming management concept based on observing, measuring and responding to inter and intra-field variability in crops. The concept of precision agriculture first emerged in the United States in the early 1980s. Crop variability typically has both a spatial and temporal component which makes statistical/computational treatments quite involved. This practice allows the farmer to vary the rate of fertilizer across the field according to the need identified by GPS guided Grid or Zone Sampling. Fertilizer that would have been spread in areas that don't need it can be placed in areas that do, thereby optimizing its use. Precision agriculture helps us to have a Decision Support System (DSS) for managing the whole farm with the ultimate goal of optimizing returns on inputs while preserving resources. Precision agriculture management practices can significantly reduce the amount of nutrient and other crop inputs used while boosting yields. Farmers thus obtain a return on their investment by saving on phytosanitary and fertilizer costs. The second, larger-scale benefit of targeting inputs in spatial, temporal and quantitative terms also concerns environmental impacts.

11.4.2 Remote Sensing

It is yet another manifestation of the application of space technologies for agriculture. Receiving information about crops at initial stages helps to take the corrective measures if situation demands so. Remote sensing is the acquisition of information about an object or phenomenon without making physical contact with the object. Sometimes it is very necessary to get an idea of the exact production after the harvest particularly when threat of surplus or shortage is expected. Remote sensing helps in monitoring the real situation and information gathered through monitoring by remote sensing can save us from a catastrophe. The system provides us with temporal as well as spatial data about different aspects.

11.5 Use of Animal Dung

Due to the scarcity of the fuels and the high costs associated with them it is necessary to look for alternative fuel. Cow manure and biogas fuel technology provides a free, sustainable source of power all year round and a useful fertilizer which helps to provide a better income for farmers. The animal dung can be used for bio gas as well as to produce dung cakes which can tremendously reduce our dependence on renewable energy source which face the threat of getting exhausted. The animal dung forms 15 per cent of the energy consumption in the rural sector. Out of the total estimated production of 324 million tonnes of animal dung (air dry), about 73 million tonnes has been estimated to be burnt for energy purposes which is more than the total fertilizer consumed in India. This animal dung if would have been used as a fertilizer it would have augmented the food production substantially besides reducing the pollution of our biosphere. As far as bio gas is concerned, a total of 31.4 lakh family size bio gas plants were set up in the country till 2000. These were producing about 3720 million cubic meters of gas per year equivalent to 2595 million tons of firewood worth rupees 439 crores.

Another benefit of the biomass is that through biomass we can get three times more energy as compared to cow dung burnt directly. In addition the plants are estimated to produce 52.5 million tonnes of enriched manure at rupees 437.5 crore per year (Singh *et al.*, 2011).

11.6 Urban Agriculture

According to the Food and Agriculture Organization, by 2020, the developing countries of Africa, Asia, and Latin America will be home to some 75 per cent of all urban dwellers. The situation in India is no different. Indian cities are home to an estimated 340 million people, almost equivalent to 30 per cent of the total population. As evident in majority of the industrialized countries, India too is experiencing a shift over time from a largely rural and agrarian population residing in villages to urban, non-agriculture centers. The Food and Agriculture Organization further estimates that by 2050 global food demand will increase by 70 per cent in order to feed the global population of 9.3 billion. This is going to put tremendous pressure on already scarce land and water resources implying an urgent need for an alternative way to combat food shortages.

Urban agriculture, although not a panacea for food insecurity, has the potential to provide millions with some secure access to food. The Food and Agriculture Organization of the United Nations has defined urban agriculture as an industry that produces, processes and markets food and fuel, largely in response to the daily demand of consumers within a town, city, or metropolis, on land and water dispersed throughout the urban and peri-urban area, applying intensive production methods, using and reusing natural resources and urban wastes to yield a diversity of crops and livestock. The CAST is an international consortium of scientific and professional societies based in Ames Iowa compiles and communicates credible science based information to policy makers, media, private sector, and the public. CAST defines urban agriculture so as to include aspects of environmental health, remediation, and recreation. It states that urban agriculture is a complex system encompassing a spectrum of interests, from a traditional core of activities associated with the production, processing, marketing, distribution, and consumption, to a multiplicity of other benefits and services such as recreation, leisure, business entrepreneurship, individual health, community health and their well being that are less widely acknowledged and documented. Urban agriculture contributes to food security and food safety.

It increases the amount of food available to people living in cities, and second, it allows fresh vegetables, fruits, and meat products to be made available to urban consumers. Urban agriculture was officially recognized by the 15th FAO-COAG session in Rome during January 1999 and subsequently at the World Food Summit in 2002. (Cited at www.fao.org/unfao/bodies/coag/coag15/x0076e).

In densely populated American cities, the use of grow-bags to raise a wide range of crops is on the rise. Many apartment dwellers with no yards or with very small yards set up these bags on a balcony or thin strip of land. Also, many types of hanging bags are available to plant, expanding the area available for planting. The bags themselves are made from a variety of materials, including canvas, weed barrier fabric, and polyester, all having semi-porous properties so the soil can drain adequately. The term "Bagri culture" was coined in 1998 by Los Angeles animator and amateur archaeologist Rudy Zappa Martinez to describe this type of agriculture. In Egypt also rooftops have been contributing in improving the family's quality of life and provide them with healthy food and raise their income. This is in addition to the environmental and aesthetic role roof top harvesting plays. In Havana, Cuba also a growing percentage of the agricultural production takes place in the so-called urban agriculture. In 2002, 35,000 acres (14,000 ha) 3,100,000 t of food. In Havana, 90 per cent of the city's fresh produce come from local urban farms and gardens.

11.6.1 City Farming

Back home in India, Dr. Doshi's city garden methods are a very good example of how the food can be produced organically for domestic consumption in reduced spaces such as terraces and balconies without requiring big investments in capital or long hours of intensive work. The food is produced from the materials available in the local environment viz sugarcane waste, polyethylene bags, tires, containers and cylinders, and soil. The containers and bags (open at both ends) are filled with the sugarcane stalks, compost, and garden soil, which make possible the use of minimal quantity of water when compared to open fields. He also recommends the idea of chain planting, or growing plants in intervals and in small quantities rather than at once and in large amounts. He has grown different types of fruit such as mangos, figs, guavas, bananas, and sugarcane stalks in his terrace of 1,200 sq ft (110 m^2) in Bandra. The concept of city farming developed by Dr. Doshi consumes the entire household's organic waste. He subsequently makes the household self-sufficient in the provision of food. About 5 kilograms of fruits and vegetables are produced daily for 300 days a year. Similarly Mumbai Port Trust has developed an organic farm on the terrace of its central kitchen, which is an area of approximately 3,000 sq ft (280 m^2). Its central kitchen distributes food to approximately 3,000 employees daily, generating important amounts of organic disposal. The terrace garden created by the staff recycles ninety per cent of this waste in the production of vegetables and fruits. In Hyderabad, it has been found that households that produce vegetables saved 20 per cent of their total food expenditures by retaining part of the produce for household consumption.

Urban agriculture may take place in locations inside the cities (intra-urban) or outside the cities in the surrounding boundaries *i.e.* peri-urban areas. The activities may take place on the homestead (on-plot) or on land away from the residence (off-plot), on private land (owned, leased) or on public land (parks, conservation areas, along roads, streams and railways), or semi-public land (schoolyards, grounds of schools and hospitals).The food products that can be obtained may be diverse from different types of grains, root crops, vegetables, mushrooms, fruits, poultry, rabbits, goats, sheep, cattle, pigs, guinea pigs, fish, etc to non-food products like aromatic and medicinal herbs, ornamental plants, tree products, etc. or combinations of these.

11.6.2 Advantages of Urban Agriculture

Easy access to fresh and nutritious food to lower income consumers

Supply to urban food markets, street food and food processing, providing additional employment and income besides providing fuel wood for urban residents and reducing urban pollution and temperatures

Water harvesting, water re-use, and urban wastes re-cycling to provide water, animal feed and fertilizers to provide for the requirements of urban agriculture

Urban agriculture helps to reduce the heat island effect. EPA defines heat island as the built up areas that are hotter than nearby rural areas. These heat islands affect communities by increasing summertime peak energy demand, air conditioning costs, air pollution and green house gas emissions. Urban agriculture can help to reduce the heat island effect. Rooftop gardens and urban farms reduce the heat absorption by pavements, rooftops and other impermeable surfaces which is main cause of increased temperature in urban areas.

Urban agriculture in India is just witnessing the beginning with few initiatives in some of the cities. These initiatives are Composting and Vermiculture; prominent in cities such as Kolkata and Chennai, Urban Agro-forestry in Hyderabad, Horticulture production activities in cities like Delhi and Terrace farming in Mumbai.

As India progresses towards a rapid phase of urbanization and as the concept of sustainable cities becomes increasingly acceptable, there are opportunities to build environmentally and economically sound urban agriculture systems, involving waste and water management that can be incorporated from the beginning itself and make it an integral part of urban planning. Urban agriculture creates a diverse ecology where fruit trees, vegetable plantations and even fishing, etc. could coexist and build a wholly ecologically sustainable scenario. In India, the concept is still at nascent stage and there is a need for greater awareness about urban agriculture. Urban agriculture has to be integrated in the agriculture policies and urban planning; and should, therefore, be brought under the purview of regulatory framework. In countries like US, China, Australia and in some European regions targets have been set up to make cities greener and sustainable. India also has to take such initiatives to promote urban agriculture which is necessary for the sustainability of its already overcrowded urban centers. (Rana Kapoor, 2013)

11.7 Bottlenecks Analysis and Interventions in Agriculture

Agriculture in India is severely hampered by various bottlenecks. These bottlenecks have severely affected the agricultural production. These bottlenecks can be minimized by providing suitable interventions thereby raising agricultural production. Raising agricultural productivity can enhance growth and employment in rural non farm sector and thereby contribute to poverty reduction. The experience from BRICS countries indicates that a one percentage growth in agriculture is more effective in reducing poverty than the same growth emanating from non-agriculture sectors. Agriculture being at the core of the development process needs to be viewed as a holistic one that of course will require suitable interventions. This will result in more employment opportunities for those who are engaged in farm as well as nonfarm activities thereby reducing the poverty and malnutrition ultimately resulting in the socio-economic upliftment of the farming community.

Based on the field study the author has analyzed bottlenecks and suggested suitable interventions. These are mentioned in Tables 30-33.

Table 30: Bottlenecks Analysis and Possible Interventions in Food Crops

Sl.No.	*Constraints*	*Causes*	*Interventions*
1.	Low yields	1. Low seed replacement ratio (SRR) 2. Use of local varieties and own seed kept during the previous year	1. Increasing Seed Replacement Ratio 2. National seeds corporation, State Seeds Corporation to produce more seeds 3. Seed Banks at the Panchayats level
2.	Non availability of fertilizers	1. Inability to estimate correctly the amount of fertilizer needed during each season 2. Total import of fertilizer from other states, lack of fertilizer plant in the state 3. Very low use of organic manures	1. Use of Organic manures 2. Production of fertilizers as perthe requirement of the states
2.	Less profit	1. High Input cost 2. High labor cost	1. Subsidy for inputs 2. Switch over to Organic farming 3. Use of Integrated methods for Disease, Pest and weed management 4. Cooperative farming
3.	Lack of credit	1. Less awareness, cumbersome process facilities	1. Increasing awareness, Use of ICT, making Procedure simpler for taking credit
4.	Lack of institutional and market linkages	1. Less extension personnel	1. Para extension workers, Diploma for Agriinput dealers to disseminate required technology and to augment extension efforts
5.	Lack of knowledge about improved varieties	1. Illiteracy 2. Less trickle down effect 3. Less use of ICT	1. Community Information Centers on the pattern e-choupals based on Hub and Spoke mechanism 2. Use of printed material, seasonal campaigns
6.	Lack of procurement facilities	1. Lack of a coherent procurement policy at the state level	1. Establishment of seasonal procurement centers for a cluster comprising 4-5 villages.
7.	Low selling price	1. Low MSP set by the government 2. Presence of middlemen	1. increase MSP *i.e.* raising it to total cost of cultivation +50 per cent 2. Emphasis on Market led Extension 3. Setting up of regulated markets

Table 31: Bottlenecks Analysis and Interventions in Livestock

Sl.No.	Nature of Bottleneck	Causes	Intervention
1	a. Low milk yield b. Late sexual maturity c. Short lactation Period	a. Local Varieties	a. Increasing stock availability through cross breeding to increase lactation period b. Motivating and facilitating small farm holders to use improved breeds of cattles
2	a. Lack of Credit and insurance facilities for livestock b. High cost of feed c. Lack of guaranteed price of the milk d. Lack of dairy processing technologies	a. Un awareness about different credit and insurance programmes b. Cumbersome process of getting credit and insurance c. Reluctance of Banks to grant loans and insurance d. Lack of Green Pastures e. No regulation on the price of milk by government	a. Encouraging Public and Private financial institutions to provide cheap loans b. Developing feed resource base including pastures, community grazing lands and other natural forages to reduce the expenses of feed c. Access to land in case of small and marginal farmers for forage d. Regulating price of milk by announcing Minimum Support Price for milk and milk products like that of food grains e. Providing value addition and food processing at the Panchayat level f. Developing projects to involve both Public and Private sector for cent per cent insurance coverage of livestock
3	a. Poor extension services regarding veterinary like vaccination b. Improper collection and distribution network c. Lack of artificial insemination facilities	a. Lack of trained men power b. Absence of cooperative organizations c. Financial constraints to provide AI centers at village or Panchayat level	a. Institutional improvements for delivery of animal health services b. Improving extension services c. Promoting a milk market expanded to the region outside the traditional centers of milk consumption

Table 32: Bottlenecks Analysis and Interventions in Horticulture

Sl.No.	Nature of Bottleneck	Causes	Intervention
1	a. Low yield of the plants b. Less profit	a. Unavailability of High Yielding varieties of fruit plants b. Lack of scientific cultivation of Plants c. Lack of value addition and fruit processing facilities	a. Ensuring availability of High yielding planting material b. Providing value addition and processing facilities c. Establishment of Post harvest infrastructure like cold storage facilities
2	a. Unavailability of Credit and insurance facilities b. High cost of inputs c. Lack of guaranteed price of the produce	a. Un awareness about different credit and insurance programmes b. Cumbersome process of getting credit and insurance c. Reluctance of Banks to grant loans and insurance d. Lack of regulated markets e. Presence of middlemen f. No price regulation by the government	a. Increasing awareness and encouraging financial institutions to provide cheap loans by setting targets for them b. Setting up of regulated markets to check middlemen c. Government to announce Minimum support price for fruit crops also
3	a. Poor extension services regarding plant diseases management, safe methods of fruit preservation and increasing the shelf life of the produce	a. Lack of required men power b. No accountability c. Lack of ICT penetration	a. Distribution of literature well in advance of the incidence of disease about its occurrence, symptoms and the controlmeasures b. Use of ICT for spreading required information c. Training to fruit growers regarding safe methods of fruit preservation and how to increase the shelf life of the produce

Table 33: Bottlenecks Analysis and Interventions in Sericulture

Sl.No.	*Nature of Bottleneck*	*Causes*	*Intervention*
1	a. Lack of rearing sheds b. High cost of Mulberry Trees	a. High cost of rearing sheds b. Scarcity of Mulberry Trees	a. Increasing Mulberry plantation on community or waste lands through social forestry programmes. b. Increasing awareness of the farmer towards different schemes for silkworm rearers for construction of rearing sheds and Mulberry Plantation
2	a. Low Profit	a. Labour intensiveness b. Large number of middlemen c. Absence of regulated market d. No post cocoon services e. Lack of any price regulation by the government	a. Establishment of seasonal regulated markets b. Provision of Post cocoon services c. Fixing a Minimum support Price on the pattern of food crops
3	a. Lack of insurance facilities for those engaged in this enterprise	a. Financial constraints of the government in providing insurance coverage to silkworm rearers	a. Provision of insurance or suitable compensation for those who are engaged in this enterprise

REFERENCES

Aggarwal, P. K., Joshi, H.C, Singh, S.D., Bhatia, A., Jain, N., Shivprasad, Choudhary, A. ,Gupta, N., Pathak, H., (2009). Agriculture and Environment, In Handbook of Agriculture, Directorate of Information and Publication, ICAR, New Delhi.

Agrawal, A (2012). Aggregating fragmented Land holdings. Agriculture Today 15(3): 49-50.

Ali, M., Gupta, S. and Basu, P. (2009). Higher levels of warming in North India will affect crop productivity. The Hindu Survey of Indian Agriculture, Chennai, India, 9-13.

Ali, Nawab (2008). Fast track to raising farm productivity. Agriculture Today, 11(10), pp: 44-45.

Anonymous (2008). Agriculture for development, World Development Report 2008. Cited at www.worldbank.org.IDA/resources/IDA/Agri.

Anonymous (2008). Report of planning commission of India. Cited at http//planningcom.nic.in/plans/five year/11th/ch/pdf.

Anonymous (2011). Union Budget and Economic Survey. 2010-11. Ministry of Finance, Government of India. New Delhi.

Anonymous (2012). Assessment of harvest and post harvest losses, Report of Central institute of Post harvest Engineering and Technology (CIPHET). Cited at http//www.ciphet.in/.

Anonymous (2012). Level of food processing in India, Cited at http//www.mofpi.nic.in.

Anonymous (2012). State of Indian Agriculture (2011-12). Government of India, Ministry of Agriculture and Cooperation, New Delhi.

Anonymous, 2001. Farming Systems and Poverty: Improving Farmers' livelihoods in a changing World. Pp: 412. Food and Agriculture organization of the United Nations, Rome.

Anonymous, 2005. A report on access to modern technologies for farming 2003, by National Sample Survey of India (NSSO), Ministry of Statistics and Programme implementation, Government of India.

Atkinson, M. D., Kettlewell, P. S., Poulton, P. R. and Hollins, P. D. (2008). Grain quality in the broadbalk wheat experiment and the winter north atlantic oscillation. Journal of Agricultural Science, Cambridge **146:** 541-549.

Awais, Mohammad and Zaidi, N. A. (2010). Domestic demand for water outstripping supply. Financing Agriculture, 42(8), pp: 10-17.

Bagchi, D. (2013). Policy debate on issue of subsidies. Employment News, 38(41): 1 and 55.

Bala Ravi S, I Hoeschle-Zeledon, MS Swaminathan and E Frison (eds) (2006) Hunger and Poverty: The Role of Biodiversity. M S Swaminathan Research Foundation and IPGRI, India and Rome, 232p.

Bandhu, D., Singh, H. and Maitra, A.K (1990). Environmental Education and Sustainable Development [ed.] Proceedings of the Third International Conference on Environmental Education. Indian Environmental Society. New Delhi. Pp: 5-9, 23-29, 61-67.

Barddhan and Tiwari, S. K. (2010). An investigation into land use dynamics in India and land under Utilization. Indian Journal of Agricultural Economics, 65(4): 658-676.

Bezemer T. M, Jones T. H.(1998). Long term effects of elevated CO2 and temperature on populations of the peach potato aphid *Myzus persicae* and its parasitoid *Aphidus matricariae*. *Oecologia*. **116**: 128–135.

Bhalla S. S and Singh, G. (2009). Final Report on Planning commission Project. Growth of Indian Agriculture, A district level study.

Bhalla, S. S. (2013) Rotting food, rotten arguments. The Indian Express, September 4.

Bharat Ramaswami (2011). Food Security Bill: would it wipe out Hunger and Poverty. Cited at irade.org/YOJANA per cent 20DECEMBER per cent 202013pdf.

Binswanger-Mkhize and Parikh, H. Indian Rural Development Report 2012-13.

Brundtland, G. H (1987). World commission on Environment and Development. Our common future, Oxford University Press, London.

Bunch, R. 1985. Two Ears of Corn: A Guide to People-Centered Agricultural improvement. Oklahoma City, Oklahoma: World Neighbors.

Chahal, T.S., Machanisation of Punjab Agriculture and its impact (Macrosd Printers, Amritsar, 1994).

Chand, R and Pandey, L. M. (2008). Discussion paper NPP 02/2008. National Center for Agricultural Economics and Applied Policy Research, ICAR, New Delhi.

Dar, D. W., Dryland Agriculture in Semi-Ari Tropics: Constraints and Opportunities. Indian Journal of Dryland Agricultural Research and Development **26**(1):1-7

Davendra, C., 2007. Small farm systems to feed hungry Asia, Outlook on Agriculture. 36(1): 7-20.

Fan, S. (2014). Enhancing Profitability of Family farms. Asia Pacific Regional Consultation, Chennai India. August, 19.

Fan, S., Gulati, A., and Sukhadeo Thorat. 2008. Investment, subsidies and pro poor growth in rural India. Agricultural Economics. 39: 1-8.

FAO (1995) Staple Foods: What do People Eat? Food and Agriculture Organization, Rome, Italy. http: //www.fao.org/ docrep/U8480E/ U8480E07.htm.

FAO (2001). Renewing SARD: Further progress towards sustainable agriculture and rural development. At http: //www.fao.org/ag/ magazine/0103sp3.htm.

Frison, E., Smith, F., Johns, T., Cherfas, J and PB Eyzaguirre (2006) Agricultural biodiversity, nutrition and health: making a difference to hunger and nutrition in the developing world. Food Nutrition Bulletin, 27(2): 167-179.

Gahukar, R.T. (2009). Food security: The challenges of Climate Change and Bio energy. Current science, 96 (1): 26-29.

Gautam H. R., (2014). Employment Opportunities in Food processing Industry for Rural Areas. Kurukshetra 62(7): 3-5.

Gautam, Raj H., and Sapehia. (2011). Need to augment irrigation capacity in agriculture. Kurukshetra, 59(4): 6-9.

Ghosh, A. (2012). Magic with Millets: Towards enhancing India's Food security. Farmer's Forum. 12(1): 29-34.

Government of India, (2008). Eleventh Five Year Plan (2007-12) Document, Volume-111, Planning commission, New Delhi.

Gulati A. (2013): In Punjab ground water level recedes daily by 33 cmdaily due to water intensive agriculture. Cited at indianexpress.com/./in-punjab-groundwater-level-recedes-by-33-cm-data.

Gulati, A. and Narayanan, S. (2003). The subsidy syndrome in Indian agriculture. Cited at ebrary.ifpri.org/cdm/ref/collection/..../181....

Gulati, Ashok (2007). Investment, subsidies and pro-poor growth in rural India, Economic and Political Weekly, 18(3),.

Gupta, A. (2012). Cultivation of vegetables in Jammu province: constraints and future strategies, Paper presented at the training programme on protected cultivation and seed production of winter vegetables, Sher-e-Kashmir University of Agricultural Sciences and Technology of Jammu, J&K.

Gupta, Anjali: (1984). Impact of agricultural subsidies, Economic and Political Weekly, 39(4) 48-53.

Halmandage, B.V. and Munde, N. N (2010). A Study of fertilizer subsidy in India, International Research Journal, 1(7): 45-50.

Haque, T. and Rake, G. (2012). LIESA India. Cited at www.agriculturesnetwork.org/...land.../....

Haverkort, B. (1995) - Agricultural Development with a Focus on Local Resources: ILEIA'S view on Indigenous Knowledge. In The Cultural Dimensions of Development: Indigenous Knowledge Systems (Eds. D. M. Warren, L. J. Slikkerveer and D. Brokensha). Intermediate Technology Publications Ltd., London, p 454 - 457.

Hazra, A. (2011). Food security in rural India: Poverty in the land of plenty, 60(5): 3-7.

Hazra, A. (2012). Adding new dimensions to sustainable rural gowth. Kurukshetra, 61(9): 1-2.

ICAR (1999). ICAR – Vision 2020, Indian Council of Agricultural Research, New Delhi, India.

IFAD, Rural Poverty Report (2011). Cited at http//www.ifad.org/rpr2011/.

IPCC (2001). Climate change, impact, adaptation and vulnerability. Contribution of working group 11 to the third assessment report of the intergovernmental panel on climate change. Cambridge University Press, Pp: 1032.

IPCC (2007). Contribution of working group III to the fourth assessment report of IPCC. (Metz, B. Davidson, O.R., Bosch, P.R., Dave. R., Meyer, L.A. (Eds.)). Cambridge University press, Cambridge, New York, USA.

Johl, S. S. (2002). Report of Expert committee on Diversification of agriculture in Punjab, Report submitted to government of Punjab, Chandigarh.

Joshi, P. K., Gulati, P. K. and Cummings, R. (Jr.) (Eds.) 2007. Agriculture Diversification and Small Holders in South Asia. Academic Foundation.

Kalkoti, G. (2013). Strategy to develop degraded land. Kurukshetra, 61(5): 26-29.

Kelkar, V. (2012). Report of the committee on Roadmap to Fiscal Consolidation. Cited at http: /finmin.nic.in/.../.

Khan, M. J (2012). Rabi crops the panacea for Ever green revolution. Agriculture Today, 15(11): 1.

Kumar, N. (2011). Agriculture needs to be in joint list of Center and all the Indian states. Crop Care. 37(2), pp: 39.

Kumar, P., Jhoshi, P. K., and Bitrhal, P. S. (2009). Demand projections for food grains in India. Agricultural Economics Research Review 22: 237-243.

Kuriakose, Francis and Iyer Kylasam Deepa. (2011). Land use and agrarian relations. Kurukshetra, 61(5): 3-9.

Lohumi, B. P. (2013). Women empowerment: Haryana shows the way. The Tribune, November 21, 2013.

Madan, M.L. (2009). Economic, social, health and environmental perspectives. The Hindu Survey of Indian Agriculture, Chennai, India, 71-75.

Mahajan, Ashwani. (2012). Need to curb diesel cars. Daily Excelsior. December 6.

Mahalingam, N. (2012). Governments claim of being pro farmer is just an eye wash. The Hindu Survey of Indian Agriculture, 66-68.

Mahapatra, I. C. (1994). Farming system research: A key to sustainable agriculture. Fertilizer News, 39(11): 13-25.

Malik, S. (2012). Why are small farmers so vulnerable in the country, The Hindu Survey of Indian Agriculture. 20-22.

Mann, S. K., 2014. Time to focus on paid ecological services, The Tribune, June 30.

Masood, A., Gupta, S. and Basu, P. S. 2009. Higher levels of warming in North India will affect crop productivity. The Hindu Survey of Indian Agriculture. The Hindu Group of Publications, pp: 44-48.

Millennium Development Goals (MDGs), India Country Report, (2011). Central Statistical Organization, Ministry of statistics and programme implementation. Cited at http//www.mospi.nic.in.

Ministry of Finance, Government of India (2011). Union Budget and Economic Survey 2010-11. New Delhi.

Mishra, P. (2013). December 2013 issue. Cited at Yojana.gov.in/.../....

Mukherjee, D., (2011). Protecting soil, Kurukshetra. June 2011.

Myers, N and Kent, J. (1995). Envirinmental exodus: an emergent crisisin the Global arena, Washington The climate institute: Washington DC.

Naoss, A. (1990). Sustainable Development and Develpment Ecology. Ethics of Environment and Development: Global Change and International Response' Edited by Engel, J. R and Engel, J. B. Belhavan Press, 25 Floral street, London.

Naylor, R. L., W. P. Falcon, R. M. Goodman, M. M. Jahn, T. Sengooba, H. Tefera and R.J. Nelson. 2004. Biotechnology in the developing world: a case for increased investments in orphan crops. Food Policy 29: 15-44.

NCAER, 1980. Implication of Tractorisation for Farm Employment, Productivity and Income. National Council of Applied Economic Research, New Delhi.

NCEUS (2008), "A Special Programme for Marginal and Small Farmers", A Report prepared by the National Commission for Enterprises in the Unorganized Sector, NCEUS, New Delhi.

Panigrahi, S. K. (2014). Environmental refugees-The result of another form of forced rural migration. Kurukshetra, **62**(11): 11-13.

Parry, M. L., Carter, T. R., and Porter, J. H., (1989). The greenhouse effect and the future of UK Agriculture. Journal of Royal Agricultural Society, 150:12-121

Patel, A. (2013). Issues facing agriculture credit in India. Cited at www.indiamicrofinance.com/issues-of-.

Pathak, H, Aggarwal, P. K, Singh and Singh, S. D. (2009). Climat Change Impact, Adoptation and mitigation in Agriculture: Methodology for Assessment and Application. Cited at www.nicra.iari.res.in/./climate per cent 20change per cent 20impact per cent 20adaptation.

Prabhu, M. J. (2012). Need to learn from Past experiences. The Hindu Survey of Indian Agriculture.14.

Prasad, C. (2011). Basic issues, experiences and futurology of agricultural extension systems in India-Implications for developing countries. Paper Published in the souvenir of International Conference on Innovative Approaches for Agricultural Knowledge management: Global Extension Experiences. November 9-12, New Delhi.

Pretty, J. N. (1995). Regenerating agriculture: Policies and Practices for sustainability and self reliance. London, England Earthscan Publications.

Raghbendra, Jha., Nagarajan, H. K., Subbarayan , P. (2005). Land Fragmentation and its Implications for Productivity: Evidence from Southern India. Australia South Asia Research Center Working Paper 2005/01

Raju, S. S., and Chand, Ramesh. 2008. NCAP Working Paper No. 8, *Agricultural Insurance in India: Problems and Prospects* National Centre for Agricultural Economics and Policy Research (Indian Council of Agricultural Research).

Rao, S. and Mishra, U. (2011). Reenergizing extension programmes to enhance fertilizer use. Available at http: /wwwkribhco.net/images/ pdf.

Reddy, Narayana (2011). Land is just not than an asset. Cited at leisaindia.org/.../LIESA-India-December

Sainath, P. (2012). The Food, the Bad and the Ugly, The Hindu, March 22.

Sarma, A., (2013). Making food security work. Kurukshetra. 62(1): 30-32.

Shanner, W. Philipp, P., and Schmehl, W. (1982). Farming Systems Research and Development: Guidelines for Developing Countries. Boulder, Colorado: West view Press.

Sharma, Davendra (2012). The Wastage Myth, Deccan Herald, November 3.

Sharma, R. 2013. Convergence and inclusive growth. In (Ed.) Kokate, K. D., Mehta, A.K., Singh, A. K, Singh Lakhan and Adhiguru, P. Future Agriculture Extension. Pp: 111-114.

Sharma, V. P. and Thaker, H. (2009). Fertilizer Subsidy in India. Cited at www.iimahd.ernet.in/./2009-07-.

Singh, Gurdev (2010). Crop Insurance in India, W. P No 2010-06-01. Research and Publication 11M-A

Singh, Gurdev. (2010). Crop Insurance in India. WP No. 2010-06-01. Indian Institute of Management Ahmadabad.

Sinha, S.K. and Swaminathan, M. S. (1991). Deforestation, Climate change and sustainable nutrition security: A case study of India. Climate change, 19: 201-209.

Sreedhar, G.(2012). A review of input and output policies for cereal production in India. Available at www.ifpri.org/sites/default/file/publications/ifpridp01159pdf.

Srinivasa Rao M, Srinivas K, Vanaja M, Rao G. G. S. N, Venkateswarlu B, Ramakrishna Y. S. (2009). Host plant (Ricinus communis Linn) mediated effects of elevated CO2 on growth performance of two insect folivores Current Science. **97**(7): 1047–1054.

Srinivasa Rao, M., Srinivas, K., Vanaja, M., Rao, G. G. S, Venkateshwarlu, B and Ramakrishna, Y. S. (2009). Host plant (Ricinus communis Linn) mediate effects of elevate carbon dioxide on growth performance of two insect Folivores. Current Science, 97:1047-1054

Srivastava, A. K. (2011). Dairy production, management and processing with particular reference to Indian farming community. In the Souvenir of 5th National Seminar of society for community mobilization on Multi sectoral innovations for rural prosperity, May 19-21, NDRI Karnal.

Stern (2005). Stern Review: The economics of Climate change. Cited at http: mudancasclimaticas.ceptac.inpe.br/.../....

Swaminathan, M. S. 2010. Need for Climate resilient agriculture. Dec.31, 2010. The Hindu. The state of Food and Agriculture: Innovation in Family Farming (2014). Food and Agriculture Organization Publications, Rome.

Tiwari, K. N. (2013). Food security-a remedy for malnutrition. Kurukshetra, 62(1): 19-23.

Tuteja, U. (2007). Indian Agriculture: In search of second green revolution. Agricultural situation in India. 64(5): 9: 15.

Uneze, Chijioke (2013). Adopting agri-preneurship education for Nigeria's quest for food security in vision 20: 2020. Greener Journal of Education and Research, **3**(9): 411-415.

USAID document (1995). Agriculture extension, rural development and food security challenge. Cited at http//www.fao.org/docrep/006/Y5061E.y5061e08.htm.

Usha Rai (2013). Rajasthan taps solar energy for agriculture, The Tribune September 20.

Vyas, S. (1996). Diversification in agriculture: concept, rationale and approaches. Indian Journal of Agricultural Economics, 51(4): 636.

Wadhwa Committee Report (2001). Cited at http// newsdawn.blogspot.com/2010/03/Wadhwa Committee.

Walker, T., (2010) Challenges and Opportunities for agricultural Research and Development in the semi arid tropics. International Crops Research Institute for the semi arid tropics, Pp: 84

Warren, D. 1991. The role of Indigenous Knowledge in facilitating a participatory approach to agricultural extension. Paper presented in: International Workshop on Agriculture Knowledge Systems and the Role of Extension, Germany. May 21-24.

WCED. (1987). Our Common Future. World Commission on Environment and Development. Oxford University Press, U.K.

INDEX

3L Model 54

A

Adaptation strategies 85
Agrarian country 66
Agri tourism 116
Agri-clinics 124
Agri-clinics and Agri-business centers (ACABC) scheme 43
Agri-ecosystem 136
Agri-preneurship 123
Agri-Tourism 115
Agribusiness 39
Agribusiness centers 124
Agricultural extension 59
Agricultural growth 6, 9
Agricultural innovation system (AIS) 59
Agricultural institutions 9
Agricultural insurance company of India (AIC) 114
Agricultural land 9
Agricultural practices 131
Agricultural Research for Development 42
Agricultural sector 40
Agricultural subsidies 16, 22
Agricultural technology 9
Agricultural technology management agency (ATMA) 60, 64
Agricultural universities 58
Agriculture 1, 41, 144
Agriculture credit 13
Agriculture infrastructure 104
Agriculture innovation systems approach 58
Agriculture markets 107
Agriculturist money lenders 15
Agripreneurs 44
Agro industries 45
Agro-climatic zones 38
Agro-processing units 8
Agroforestry 37

Agronomic approaches 37
AIDIS 14
Animal dung 151
Animal husbandry 1
Antodya anna yojana (AAY) 49
Apiary 90
Attracting and retaining youth in agriculture (ARYA) 43

B

Bacillus thuringiensis 109
Bagri culture 153
Bank credit 36
Biofertilizers 37
BRICS 74
Broad based extension 59
Bt cotton 110

C

Cacia fistula 134
CACP 12
Cannabis sativa 133
Carbon dioxide 80
CAST 153
Cattle 155
Center for sustainable agriculture 3
Cereals 3, 32
Certified emission reduction (CER) 148
CH_4 85
Chemical fertilizers 131
CIPHET 32
City farming 154
Climate change 78, 80, 81
Climate risk management research and training centre 87
Climate risk managers 88
Climatic conditions 2
CO_2 81, 85, 145
Commercial banks 15
Community grain storage banks 51
Community participation 39
Community property resources (CPR) 39
Cooperative credit societies act 15
Cooperative farming 120
Cooperative society 58
Cotton 21
Crop diversification 85, 94
Crop insurance 111
Crop intensification techniques 13
Crop production 134
Cropped area 19, 20
Cropping intensity 98
Crops 21
CSTEP 149
Cultivators 42
Cyclone 113

D

Dairy 90
Dairy products 31
Dairy sector 29
DDT 146
Decision support system (DSS) 151
DEFRA 91
Department for environment, food and rural affairs 90
Diversification 13, 37, 89, 92
DNA 108
Drinking water 82

Drip irrigation 102, 106
Dry land 34

E

e-choupals 106
e-PDS 53
Ecological services 134
Economic growth 66
Electronic public distribution supply chain management 53
Eleusine coracana 122
Employment generation 94
Export potential 93
Extension 3
Extension functionaries 67
Extension services 9, 56, 66

F

FAO 73
Farm communities 58
Farm income insurance scheme 114
Farm mechanization 29, 99
Farm size 19
Farm women 9
Farmer community 118
Farmer field schools 66
Farmer trainers extension 65
Farmer's forum global meeting 43
Farmers interest groups (FIGs) 69
Farmers producer organizations (FPOs) 69
Farmers rights act 139
Farmers' suicides 5
Farming community 42
Farming system approach 91
Fate of the farmer 3
Fertilizer 2, 19, 23, 25, 38
Fertilizer subsidy 17, 18
Fertilizer subsidy policy 20
Fertilizer use 19
Fish 155
Fisheries 32
Focusing small farmers 95
Fodder shortage 35
Food and agriculture organization 152
Food corporation of India (FCA) 10, 33, 48, 53
Food coupons 52
Food crops 21
Food grains 18, 26, 36, 70, 72
Food grains production 2, 7
Food grains storage 55
Food packaging 147
Food processing 29, 46, 102
Food security 34, 129
Food security act 22, 75
Food stamps 50
Food subsidy 17, 22
Food wastage 32
Forest conservation law 135
FRA 138
Fruits 31, 155

G

Genetic modification 110
Genetically modified organisms (GMO) 108, 148
GHGs emissions 83
Global agriculture 6
Global hunger report 2014 10

Global warming 80
GM foods 109
Grain drain 10, 33, 103
Great Himalayan national park 135
Green house gases (GHGs) 78, 80, 85
Green revolution 132
Gross domestic product (GDP) 6, 17, 73, 123
Gross State domestic product (GSDP) 54

H

Hailstorm 113
Haiti 23
Harvesting 31
Horticulture 124
HUNGaMA 4
Hurricane 113
Hydrofluorocarbons 80

I

ICAR-SAUs 8
ICICI-Lombard general insurance company 114
ICRISAT 86
ICT-enabled tools 60
IFFCO-Tokio general insurance company 114
Illusive growth rate 6
Indian council of agricultural research (ICAR) 3, 38, 56, 128
Indian economy 16
Indian farmers 1
Indian tobacco company (ITC) 60, 106
Indigenous technical knowledge (ITK) 59, 132
Information communication technology (ICT) 60, 106
Infrastructure 55
Innovations in technology dissemination (ITD) 60
Insect pests 83
Institute of applied manpower research (IAMR) 41
Integrated techniques 130
Intensification 102
Interlinking 143
International assessment of agricultural knowledge 127
International food policy research institute (IFPR) 49
International monetary fund 24
Interventions 156
Investment 26, 45
IPCC 85
IPM 59
Irrigation 2, 31, 39
Irrigation capacity 101

K

KCC 16
Kelkar Committee 17
Krishi vigyan kendra (KVK) 57

L

Labour productivity 36
Labourers 42
Land productivity 36
Land use 27
Livestock 35, 84, 90, 124
Livestock insurance scheme 114
Livestock productivity 35

M

Macro nutrients 21

Macroeconomic policy 128

Mahatma Gandhi National rural Employment Guarantee Act (MGNREGA) 38, 51

Manihot esculenta 122

Market led extension 65

Meat 31, 32

Mechanization 31

Medicinal plants 39

Methane 80

Milk 32

Millennium development goals (MDGs) 72

Minimum support prices (MSP) 12, 13

Ministry of agriculture and cooperatives 56

Mitigation strategies 85

Modern agriculture 121

MS Swaminathan foundation limited 60

Multi commodity exchange of India (MCX) 141

Mushrooms 155

N

N_2O 85

NABARD 118

Nano sensors 147

Nanoemulsions 147

Nanofertilizers 144

Nanofood 146

Nanomedicines 146

Nanotechnology 144, 146, 147

National advisory council 72

National agricultural insurance scheme (NAIS) 113

National board of trade (NBOT) 141

National commodity and derivatives exchange limited 141

National farmers commission 107

National food security act 54

National horticultural board 105

National mission on agricultural extension and technology 68

National multi commodity exchange (NMCE) 141

National perspective plan (NPP) 143

National sample survey 56

National sample survey organization (NSSO) 11, 14, 41, 50

National wasteland development board 103

National water development agency (NWDA) 143

Natural resource management 59

Natural resources 36.

Newspaper 58

NGO 6, 57, 64, 69

Nitrous 80

Nitrous oxide 80

NSA 27

Nutrition barometer 6

Nymphela depunctalis 133

O

Oilseeds 32

Organic farming 59, 131

Organic matter 38
Organic products 39
Ornamental plants 155
Orphan crops 121
Oxfam 24

P

Paddy growing farmers 4
Panchayat food grains 51
Panchayati raj institutions 39
Panicum sumatrense 122
Payments for ecosystem services (PES) 134
Pectinophora gossypiella 83
Phosphatic 20
Photosynthetic 145
Piggery 90
Pigs 155
Planning commission 3, 7, 26
Plant protection 31
Policy makers 17
Population 26, 54, 76
Population density 36
Post liberalization periods 21
Potashic fertilizers 20
Poultry 31, 32, 90, 155
Poverty 66, 70, 73
Poverty ratio 36
PPV 138
Precision farming 150
Primary agricultural cooperative societies (PACS) 15
Processing 147
Protecting farmers' rights 138
Protection of plant varieties 139
Public distribution system (PDS) 10, 11, 33, 34, 48, 52, 103
Public extension worker 58
Public private partnership (PPP) 64
Pulses 2, 25, 32, 84

R

Rabbits 155
Radio 58
Rainfall insurance scheme 114
Rainfall pattern 79
Rainfed 7
Rainfed agriculture 29, 34, 35
Rainfed areas 38
Rainwater 1
Rapeseed mustard 21
Rashtriya krishi bima yojana (RKBY) 113
RAWE 43
Remote sensing 151
Renewable energy 148
Renewable energy rources 148
Resource-conserving technologies (RCTs) 36, 86
Reuters market lights (RML) 60
Revamped PDS (RPDS) 48
Rice 45
Right to food 75
Rivers 8
Rural credit survey report 14
Rural development 51
Rural entrepreneurship and awareness development 43
Rural households 45
Rural infrastructure 18

S

Satellite farming or site specific crop management 151
Sea level 78
Self help groups 118
Semi urban areas 46
Sericulture 90
Setaria itallica 122
Shrimps 31
Small farmers' agribusiness consortium (SFAC) 65
Social initiatives group (SIG) 114
SOFA 2014 136
Soil 83
Soil erosion 94
Soil health improvement 134
Soil profile 20
Solar energy 148
Sprinkler irrigation 106
Strong precise delivery systems 146
Sub mission on agricultural mechanization (SMAM) 68
Sub mission on plant protection and plant quarantine 68
Sub-mission on agricultural extension (SMAE) 68
Sub-mission on seed and planting material (SMSP) 68
Subsidy 21
Sugarcane 21
Suicides 5
Supplemental mutritional assistance programme 51
Sustainable agricultural development 126
Sustainable agriculture 130
Sustainable development 128
Sustainable intensification 130
System of crop intensification (SCI) 131

T

Targeted public distribution scheme (TPDS 12
Tata economic consultancy 11, 33, 49
Tata kissan sanchar limited 60
Technical efficiency 120
Television 58
Temperatures 80
Tempest 113
The cooperative credit societies act 15
The food and agriculture organization 24
Threshers 31
Tillage 31
Total factor productivity (TFP) 26
Tractor 31
Tropical plateau 35
Typhoon 113

U

UN DESA 73
UN FAO 10
UNICEF 127
Unirrigated areas 20
Universal distribution system 52
Urban agriculture 152, 155
USAID 6, 73
USDA 128

V

Vegetable plantations 155
Vegetables 3
Vigna umbellate 122
Vigna unguiculata 122

W

Wadhwa committee 11
Wastage 32
Wasteland 103
Water 82
Water management 155
Water use efficiency 102
Weather 87
Weather based crop insurance scheme (WBCIS) 114
Wheat 3, 21, 45
Wind power 148, 149
World bank 13
WTO 76, 139

Y

Youth in agriculture 43